THE OLD DUTCH CHURCH OF SLEEPY HOLLOW

LEGENDS AND LORE OF THE OLDEST CHURCH IN NEW YORK

CURRIER & IVES, 1867

The Old Dutch Church of Sleepy Hollow

Legends and Lore of the Oldest Church in New York

Janie Couch Allen and Elinor Griffith

Photography by Lyle Anderson and Janie Couch Allen

CONTENTS

ACKNOWLEDGMENTS

DANK JE WEL!

A new pastor, ambitious plans and a timeline so tight that the 325th celebration must have been God-inspired …

Only months after his arrival in 2009 and within days of the start of the New Year in 2010—the church's 325th anniversary—Rev. Jeffrey Gargano teamed up with Aubrey Hawes, president of the Friends of Old Dutch, and church members Janie Allen, Lillian Hess, and sexton and elder John Paine. A grand vision of how to celebrate the Old Dutch captured their imagination.

Dozens of volunteers pitched in, and a yearlong series of special events took shape: a spring reception, the launch of an innovative iPad tour of the historic site, a concert by renowned organist Kent Tritle, a gala reception and more. This book, first published in 2011, came out of that collaboration, too.

The book design is the creation of Christopher Vaccaro of the New Castle Media Center. Its executive director, Carrie Krams, graciously allowed us to use the computer facilities. Special assistance also came from Susan Doremus (research) and Jeanette Gingold (proofreading). Moreover, the book's research and photos benefited enormously from Historic Hudson Valley (collections manager Jessa Krick, librarian Catalina Hannan, former curator Kate Johnson and PR director Rob Schweitzer).

These folks helped us round out our knowledge of the important role of the Old Dutch: Rick Hessney; Sexton Emeritus William Lent; Sleepy Hollow Cemetery's Jim Logan; Dave Logan; Sara Mascia, curator of the Historical Society Serving Sleepy Hollow and Tarrytown; Marcia Moore; librarian Patrick Raftery of the Westchester County Historical Society; Evelyn Schlauch; Sleepy Hollow village historian Henry Steiner; Rev. Gerald and Barbara Vander Hart; and New Castle village historian Gray Williams.

An unexpected resource deserves special recognition: the Netherlands Consulate General in New York. Former Consul General Hugo Gajus Scheltema, editor of *Exploring Historic Dutch New York*, agreed to write the book's introduction, about the Dutch in early America.

And *dank je wel,* our special thanks to you, the book's readers, for your interest in this historical jewel, the Old Dutch Church of Sleepy Hollow.

— AAG ASSOCIATES

> "A CHURCH STANDS IN A COMMUNITY FOR A BLESSING TO THAT COMMUNITY."
>
> —REV. ARTHUR MABON, SECOND REFORMED CHURCH, 1901

PREFACE

BEFRIENDING THE OLD DUTCH

The Old Dutch Church and Burying Ground of Sleepy Hollow, built in 1685, is perched on a knoll overlooking the trickling Pocantico River, which meanders down to the Hudson. This idyllic place, the setting for Washington Irving's "Legend of Sleepy Hollow" is just twenty-five miles north of the cacophony of Manhattan's Times Square. It has befriended congregants and people of all faiths for over 300 years. Virtually every resident in surrounding communities claims an affinity.

The Friends of Old Dutch, a not-for-profit group organized in 1985, shares a special affinity with this historic place, New York's oldest church. Our mission is to help in the restoration and preservation of the church and burying ground. Our newest undertaking has been to help to create easier access to this local treasure.

Historically, to enter the church required just two small steps. Over the years the road in front of the church was lowered by ten feet. As a result, entry required scaling seven somewhat treacherously uneven steps. It made access virtually impossible for people who were physically challenged.

Working with the congregation, the Friends engaged an architectural firm noted for its award-winning work related to historic buildings. The architectural plans permitted access to Old Dutch without the challenge of a single step! Construction began in March 2017 and was completed in June, in time for the summer worship season.

We give a very special acknowledgement to Janie Couch Allen, who guided the second edition of this delightful book. We also wish to recognize the contributions of Lyle Anderson and Elinor Griffith who with Ms. Allen planned, wrote, edited and photographed the first edition. They captured the history of this legendary church known locally as Old Dutch.

Today the Friends of Old Dutch remain committed to our preservation efforts so that future generations may have the opportunity to befriend this registered National Historic Landmark.

We give a most special thanks to all those friends of Old Dutch who have supported our efforts with financial contributions over the years. Without your support we cannot continue to help with the restoration, preservation and improved access to this wonderful treasure.

AUBREY HAWES,
PRESIDENT
FRIENDS OF OLD DUTCH

INTRODUCTION

DUTCH FOOTSTEPS IN EARLY AMERICA

The first church leaders in the colony were colorful people who came in the early 1600s, long before the Old Dutch Church of Sleepy Hollow was even a dream. Amateur historian Hugo Gajus Scheltema, former consul general of the Netherlands in New York, has visited the Old Dutch, "peeping into the windows and reading Dutch headstones." "The important role that the Dutch Reformed Church played in those formative days is striking," he says. Here are his observations on how the church was such a vital player in the New Netherland colony.

In the seventeenth century, comfort was often the most one could give to ill people in physical or mental distress. Such comfort came, obviously, from the Holy Scriptures and thus a *ziekentrooster,* or comforter of the sick, was also a lay minister. He performed basic religious duties and looked after the religious needs of the population in the absence of an official minister. He served as a schoolmaster too.

Bastiaen Jansz Krol (or Crol) was such a *ziekentrooster*. Having arrived in New Netherland in 1624 from Friesland in the north of the Dutch Republic, he was the first person to perform religious services in the young colony, in accordance with the practices of the Dutch Reformed Church. The small Dutch congregation initially met in a mill on a small muddy road, which was appropriately called *Slycksteeg,* now Mill Street in Manhattan. Interestingly, the very same upper floor of the mill was subsequently used for the first Jewish religious meetings.

Hugo Gajus Scheltema studying Dutch documents in the state archives in Albany, N.Y.
Photo courtesy H. G. Scheltema.

INTRODUCTION (CONTINUED)

Krol was also active at Fort Orange, the early Dutch fort at present-day Albany, N.Y., and did well enough to succeed Pieter Minuit as an interim director of New Netherland in 1632.

In 1628, the first proper Protestant minister, called *domine*, was Jonas Michaëlius. He established the first Dutch Reformed Church in New Netherland, the predecessor of the Collegiate Church of Manhattan. Michaëlius was soon followed by others, in Flatbush and elsewhere on Long Island, in Beverwijck (Albany) and along the Hudson River, including Kingston. Among the most fascinating of these *domine*s were Everardus Bogardus and Johannes Megapolensis. Both were strong personalities playing important roles in establishing an often uneasy balance between the local government and the colonists. Indeed, many early ministers had clashes with the local government over public affairs, obviously long before separation between state and church became the norm.

In the early 1600s New Netherland needed every hand it could get from Europe to build a strong counterweight to the pressuring English neighbors, and could not be choosy. A stern Protestant, Petrus Stuyvesant, the last of the Dutch directors, tried to establish structure in the young communities. But it was too late. In 1664, Stuyvesant signed the Articles of Transfer allowing New Netherlanders to "keep and enjoy the liberty of their consciences in religion" and the English took over, only to have the Dutch regain the territory temporarily until it was permanently ceded in 1674.

Fortunately, the string of Dutch churches in America—roughly thirteen by 1664—could remain, and new ones could be built, such as the Old Dutch Church of Sleepy Hollow. These churches remain as historical jewels, truly shining and vibrant vestiges of the Dutch footprint in America. Little is left of those early churches; often Dutch-inscribed tombstones provide the only clear reference to these early days.

For me, however, the Old Dutch is one of the churches that come closest to the Dutch heritage. One has only to peek through the windows to imagine oneself in a typical Dutch village church—which is one of the reasons I so often come back to that wonderful place.

CHAPTER 1

THREE CENTURIES
AND COUNTING

Vibrant and vital, tranquil beyond compare, the Old Dutch Church of Sleepy Hollow continues today on its legendary journey through American history. More than three centuries ago, its stone walls were sturdily laid, its bell from Holland lovingly placed in the belfry, and its industrious and pious congregation—a few poor families, backed by their very wealthy patron Frederick Philipse, who would soon become the lord of Philipsburg Manor—began gathering to worship. This humble building is now New York's oldest church and one of the oldest in the country.

A Dutch Treat! Well into the late 1700s, Dutch was spoken from the pulpit of this church, which is a National Historic Landmark.
Photos: Church at Christmas, preceding page and above, Moira Gargano.

A Church for All Times—and All Seasons

In a span of time approaching four centuries since 1685, God's presence has graced the Old Dutch Church and its congregation. Informing, encouraging, guiding, comforting, loving … and sheltering.

"Yet ironically much of the church's rich past appears to have nothing to do with religion," says Rev. Jeffrey Gargano, the enthusiastic pastor of the Old Dutch Church and the Reformed Church of the Tarrytowns. "The little church was where Gen. George Washington rested weary from war or where a teenaged Washington Irving frolicked among the tombstones and later set much of 'The Legend of Sleepy Hollow.' It's known for the artistry of its carved folk-art gravestones."

In short, this holy place is also a well-known literary, historical and cultural landmark that draws thousands of people annually to its unpretentious door.

Over the years the Old Dutch Church has welcomed all knocks at that door: the Dutch miller, French Huguenot farmer and enslaved African; the highfalutin lord of the manor; the mischievous, giggling teen (soon a world-famous writer) and the exhausted general (soon America's first president); and now the banker, biker and immigrant. It even welcomes imaginary knocks at night … of ghosts and goblins, and a Headless Horseman. Welcomes curious tourists too. They freely roam the church and burying grounds, learn about its legends and lore, and then linger in its serenity. They come from the United States and places as distant as Holland, Afghanistan and New Zealand. And following a tour of this enchanting place, many visitors pen hearty words of thanks in the church guest book.

Some others, the locals, have a more permanent relationship and are thankful to know the church in all its seasons—the candlelit Christmas service, the solemn Service of Shadows on Good Friday and Easter sunrise celebration among the graves, summertime sermons and music, joyous baptisms and weddings, and, of course, funerals. And the autumn—oh, yes, the autumn, with those spine-tingling October evenings around Halloween when "The

"IT STANDS ON A KNOLL, SURROUNDED BY LOCUST TREES AND LOFTY ELMS, FROM AMONG WHICH ITS DECENT, WHITEWASHED WALLS SHINE MODESTLY FORTH, LIKE CHRISTIAN PURITY, BEAMING THROUGH THE SHADES OF RETIREMENT. A GENTLE SLOPE DESCENDS FROM IT TO A SILVER SHEET OF WATER, BORDERED BY HIGH TREES, BETWEEN WHICH, PEEPS MAY BE CAUGHT AT THE BLUE HILLS OF THE HUDSON."

—WASHINGTON IRVING, "THE LEGEND OF SLEEPY HOLLOW," 1819–20

Wedded Bliss. Ever since the first recorded Dutch marriage in 1698, marriages like this one, for Daniela and Russ Anello, have enlivened this little church. Photo: Michelle Shirley.

> ANY CHURCH STANDING BY THE WAYSIDE, NO MATTER HOW PLAIN OR HUMBLE, IS A SUGGESTIVE THING. WE READ THAT A SHIP WAS WRECKED UPON THE REEFS OF AN ISLAND IN THE PACIFIC, AND THAT THE SAILORS FEARED THEY MIGHT FALL INTO THE HANDS OF SAVAGE MEN. ONE CLIMBED A HILL TO RECONNOITER, AND FROM HIS OUTLOOK SHOUTED BACK: 'COME ON, BOYS; HERE'S A CHURCH!'
>
> "THAT SPIRE TOLD THEM AT ONCE THEY WERE SAFE; TOLD THEM, TOO, THAT HERE MUST BE INTELLIGENCE, COMFORT, AND CIVILIZATION. ANY CHURCH WILL SIGNIFY AS MUCH AS THAT, BUT THAT LITTLE OLD BUILDING, WHICH STANDS WITH THE HUDDLED GRAVES CROWDING CLOSE UP TO ITS WALLS, HAS AN ADDED INTEREST. IT CARRIES OUR THOUGHTS BACK TO WHEN IT WAS FOUNDED."
>
> —REV. JOHN KNOX ALLEN, 1918

Legend" is once again enacted and wise people watch their step carefully in the Old Dutch Burying Ground.

Whether new to the community or a member of the church, whether a tourist or a frolicking, sporting, boyish whipster (in Irving's words), each person has a very personal experience at the Old Dutch, hopefully spiritual and likely literary, historical and cultural as well.

For countless years to come, may its welcoming "whitewashed walls shine modestly forth, like Christian purity" and grace the lives of all who enter its door!

A Spellbinding Tale. As October leaves rustle outside, Jonathan Kruk enacts "The Legend." Photo: Todd Attebury for Historic Hudson Valley.

Life at the Old Dutch. From concerts by renowned organist Kent Tritle and other musical events to the echoing hoofbeats of the Headless Horseman, even enchanting tales from volunteers and a bit of fun at the Tarrytown Halloween Parade, the little church continues to thrive.

Photos: Church at Christmas, preceding page and above, Moira Gargano.

TOUCHING HOLINESS

Rev. Jeffrey Gargano, pastor of the Old Dutch Church, reflects on the church's spiritual role over the years.

"To know Christ, and to make him known." That phrase appeared on every Sunday bulletin of the church I grew up in. I guess that is about as obvious and meaningful a statement of mission as any church could proclaim ... and in ten words or less! That's been our challenge at the Old Dutch Church of Sleepy Hollow for more than 300 years and will continue, God willing, for at least 300 more years.

When all is said and done, when choir practice is over, when the closing prayer is prayed, when the benediction is pronounced, we ought to be able to look back over those moments of song or prayer or religious reflection and understand deeply how Christ has been revealed and praised in what we have done. And that "knowing of Christ" has happened since the first service.

It's the second part of the expression, "to make Christ known," that requires more effort on our part. I, perhaps like you, struggle with this in much of the daily comings and goings of life. (This is especially true for me when behind the wheel of a car, as in years past it must have been for people sitting in a slow-moving, horse-drawn buggy.) But in so many ways our little church finds opportunities to live out its purpose, Christ's purpose. For this is the place where God's word took hold along the Lower Hudson Valley, and from this church other churches were given birth.

A Pastor for All Seasons. Rev. Jeffrey Gargano

But there's more, as I discovered, on how this simple stone edifice has always appeared to have a seemingly mystical connection to the divine. Let me explain…

Several years ago, when I learned I was to come to the Old Dutch Church, I thought a re-reading of "The Legend of Sleepy Hollow" would be a pretty good idea. The basic contours of the story were familiar enough, but the details? Well, if you haven't read it recently, pick it up again soon. Maybe because I was about to serve the church, its role in the story took on a heightened profile. You'll remember that as schoolmaster Ichabod Crane is racing to evade the villain, it is the vision of the church that encourages … if he can just gallop across the bridge into the churchyard, then he will be safe. The Old Dutch Church is safety, shelter, sanctuary.

Sunrise Service. The Old Dutch's atmosphere has a lightness, a sense of hope, on Easter morning.

In Celtic spirituality there is a notion that there are places on this green earth where the membrane that separates the temporal from the eternal is very thin. Thin Places. The Holy Land must be like that. And Stonehenge. Come to the Old Dutch Church at dusk in the autumn, or on a candlelit Christmas Eve, as shadows from the limbs of a tree outside dance across the whitewashed walls. The atmosphere at the Old Dutch Church can feel very thin. You can almost touch holiness.

For over three centuries this mystical "thinness" and holiness may help explain why so many people have been drawn to this venerable church, from early Dutch farmers who traveled over rough trails to reach it; to Irving, who never forgot his boyhood visits; to thousands of tourists who arrive each year. It may explain why it survived when other churches were destroyed in the Revolutionary War. Why it was brought back after a fire caused by lightning, and why it prospered when larger churches were built nearby. Members refused to abandon it. They experienced the thinness. And they return every summer "to know Christ and to make him known."

Truly, this little church and its people have been such major players in our nation's political, literary and spiritual life. All big things. Perhaps most important, though, is the outsize role that this small church continues to play in our village life. In the very narrowest sense of church membership, well, the church doesn't have many members. But in a much broader sense, everyone who lives in our villages or enters its sacred doors enjoys membership—and that means you too.

Sure, it is a place of history and legends and lore, but most of all the Old Dutch Church of Sleepy Hollow is God's place—a Thin Place. A place of safety and shelter and sanctuary and holiness.

Si Deus Pro Nobis, quis Contra Nos? (Romans 8:31, If God is for us, who can be against us?)

—Inscription on the Old Dutch Church Bell, 1685

THE OLD DUTCH CHURCH OVER THE YEARS

1609 *Henry Hudson sailed up the Hudson River*

1624 *New Netherland colony formed by Dutch Republic*

1626 *Dutch acquired Manhattan Island from Lenape native Americans for goods worth 24 dollars (60 guilders)*

1664 *Dutch surrendered to British; colony renamed New York*

1681 *Frederick Philipse purchased the Pocantico River Valley from Lenape native Americans and built Upper Mills*

1685 *Frederick Philipse built the Old Dutch Church*

Serene in Sleepy Hollow. In his 1886 *History of Westchester County*, John Thomas Scharf included this engraving of the Old Dutch Church.

1697 *Organized as a Reformed Protestant Dutch Church*

1702 *Lord Philipse died: 200 people on the manor; Upper Mills bequeathed to son Adolph; Lower Mills to grandson Frederick II*

1715 *Church compiled its First Record Book*

1730 *Lady Catherine died; left silver beaker and table to church*

1750 *Nearly 1,000 on the manor, including 23 slaves; Adolph Philipse died; Philipsburg Manor reunited under Frederick II*

1751 *At death of Frederick II, church and manor inherited by Frederick III, who auctioned slaves and leased out Upper Mills*

1755 *Elizabeth Guion died; currently the churchyard's oldest legible grave marker*

1776–1783 *Revolutionary War (Frederick III sided with British)*

1779 *New York State charged Frederick III with treason, confiscated Philipsburg Manor; after the war he fled to England*

1781 *Gen. Washington and the Continental Army rested at the church on July 2*

1785 *First full-time minister, Stephen Van Voorhees, shocked the congregation by baptizing Levine Hawes in English*

1787 *Church consistory received church deed*

1819–20 *Washington Irving published "The Legend of Sleepy Hollow"*

1837 *A fire caused by lightning damaged the church; repairs included a new entrance with portico; new church built in Tarrytown*

1851 *Some Old Dutch members left to organize the Second Reformed Church in Tarrytown*

1854 *New church built in North Tarrytown (now Sleepy Hollow) for the Old Dutch congregation; it was called First Reformed Church*

1863 *Pastor Abel Stewart confronted draft rioters intent on burning Tarrytown*

1874 *North Tarrytown (now Sleepy Hollow) incorporated*

1897 *200th anniversary of the church's organization: Theodore Roosevelt, speaker*

1961 *National Historic Landmark designation*

1991 *The First and Second Churches reunited to form the Reformed Church of the Tarrytowns*

2010 *Old Dutch's 325th anniversary celebration*

CHAPTER 2

THE LORD OF THE MANOR
AND HIS CHURCH,
1685–1702

n 1609, Henry Hudson became the first European to explore the river that bears his name. Soon this bountiful wilderness beckoned Dutch fur traders, and a thriving trade grew up between the pioneers and the natives. Within decades, the river teemed with watercraft hauling all kinds of cargoes, from beaver pelts, timber and salted sturgeon to livestock and even summer peaches. Late in the century, the richest man in Manhattan boarded a river sloop. His destination? A bay twenty miles north of the island, where a swift stream the natives called the Pe-kan-ti-ko—"a run between two hills"—drained into the Hudson. His destiny? Lord of an expansive new manor.

Summoning Worshippers for Centuries. The 1685 bell, cast to order in the Netherlands, still rings for Sunday worship services each summer.

Frederick Philipse Builds a Church

Around 1682, a ship brought Frederick Philipse, fifty-six, a Dutch immigrant who had established himself as one of New York's most prominent citizens, up the Hudson River to its broadest stretch. Dutch sailors called the three-mile-wide expanse the Tappan Zee, after a tribe of Indians living on the west bank. The ship dropped anchor in the picturesque bay on the east side called Slaepershaven, or Sleepy Haven. Philipse's attention was drawn to hills thick with virgin forest. His interest lay not so much in the timber as in the rich, loamy soil. It was ideal for growing wheat. And wheat flour, as the savvy merchant knew, was in high demand by the British military and Caribbean sugar plantations.

He had recently bought this valley from Lenape native Americans, who had hunted, fished and farmed the area for generations. Just as Peter Minuit had bought Manhattan Island from the natives in 1626 for 60 guilders' worth ($24) of beads and goods, Philipse negotiated a deal with the *sachems*, or chiefs, that included:

> *10 fathoms of duffils [60 feet of cloth]; 10 blankets; 8 gunns, 7 shirts; 1 anker [10 gallons] of rum; 25 lbs. of powder; 10 bars of lead; 2 iron potts, 5 earthen cans, 12 steeles to strike fire, 2 coopers' adz, 2 half vatts of beere, 7 pairs of stockings, 6 howes; 12 axes; 9 kettles; 40 knives; 6 brass tobacco boxes; 6 coates; 2 drawing knives, and 70 fathoms of wampum.*

Philipse speculated in the Indian currency wampum, or strung shell beads, each a quarter-inch long and painstakingly cut from shells found in Long Island Sound. To drive up its value, he sometimes stockpiled hogsheads of wampum in his cellars. The unit of measure was the fathom, six-foot lengths of woven bands or belts of the strung beads. So, to buy the land, Philipse had no problem getting together seventy fathoms, or 420 feet, of wampum, which required about 20,000 beads to make and was worth about 125–140 guilders.

Now Philipse followed the Pocantico River a short distance upstream to the site of an old mill, which had served a small community of farmers earlier in the century. His building plan began to take shape.

" IT IS NOT DIFFICULT TO IMAGINE HOW FREDERICK PHILIPSE APPEARED. HE WAS A TALL AND WELL-PROPORTIONED MAN; HAD A QUIET GRAY EYE, A ROMAN NOSE, AND FIRM SET MOUTH. DRESSED IN THE COSTUME OF THE PERIOD WITH FULL EMBROIDERY, LACE CUFFS, ETC., AND HEAD SURMOUNTED WITH IMPRESSIVE PERIWIG AND FLOWING RINGLETS, HE MOVED WITH A SLOW AND MEASURED STEP, WHICH GAVE HIM AN AIR OF DIGNITY. IN TEMPERAMENT, HE WAS GRAVE AND MELANCHOLY, AND SO RETICENT AS TO BE REGARDED DULL; AND WHILE INTELLIGENT, AND SHREWD ALMOST TO CRAFTINESS, HE IS SAID NOT TO HAVE BEEN ESPECIALLY CULTURED."

—AMERICAN SCENIC & HISTORIC PRESERVATION SOCIETY, 1908

Upper Mills. The Philipsburg Manor gristmill and manor house, built by Frederick Philipse and later enlarged, are open to the public. Photo: Historic Hudson Valley.

He would construct a dam and a gristmill at the site of the old miller's house, as well as a sawmill, a trading post and a wharf for shallow-draft river boats. A new stone house would serve as an administrative center, with a bedroom for when he came up from the family residence in New York.

Philipse named the venture Upper Mills to distinguish it from his operations at Lower Mills, in Yonkers, where he had a gristmill operation and summer home. Upper Mills would help to give Philipse what every good Dutch businessman desired: control over supply, production, transport and marketing. And profits ...

> **Upper Mills was an ambitious scheme, but Frederick Philipse had bigger dreams.**

It was an ambitious scheme, but well within the means of Frederick Philipse. He had already achieved more than most men dreamed of. With his wife and business partner,

Margaret, he had created a vast shipping and trading empire. His was the rags-to-riches story to beat.

Philipse's origins were modest. His father was Philippus Douwes, a roof slater, and his mother was Ebel Fedricks. They lived in Bolsward, a village in the northern Dutch province of Friesland. Town archives record that Philipse was baptized Fedrick (his name was later Anglicized) on March 8, 1627. His elder brother continued the family business, so in 1653 Frederick, twenty-seven, immigrated to New Amsterdam, as New York City was called. He went to work for the Dutch West India Company as a master carpenter.

A bustling town with nearly 1,000 residents, New Amsterdam offered the ambitious lad many opportunities. In 1657, he dropped his tools and joined the merchant class. Claiming the "small burgherright" (citizenship, with trade privileges) from the municipal government, he chartered his first ship to pick up tobacco in Virginia. Soon he was buying furs upriver, wines in Manhattan and land in Yonkers.

He proved to be as lucky in love as he was in business. In 1662, he married Margaret Hardenbroeck, the rich widow of a rival merchant, and a ship owner in her own right.

When the British coerced the Dutch to hand over the colony of New Netherland in 1664, Philipse swore allegiance to the Crown, and carried on business as usual. His ships ranged over the oceans to Europe, the West Indies and Africa, trading goods that yielded the highest profits: furs, lumber, molasses, tobacco, rum. A decade later he was the richest person in New York City.

The Pocantico River Valley, with its potential for a lucrative wheat-flour trade, actually meant more to Philipse than just a moneymaking venture. His larger ambition? He wanted a manor for himself. Manors, created by royal patent, were springing up in New York: Fordham Manor to the south and Pelham Manor on Long Island Sound. The king hoped the patentees—a few wealthy landowners— would bring in new settlers as tenants, thus increasing his tax revenues. Owners benefited from the right to establish terms for tenant leases, collect rents and settle tenant disputes. And a patent granted an owner the title of "Lord."

In 1680, Charles II had granted Philipse the right to amass landholdings in the lower Hudson Valley. Philipse already owned more than 7,000 acres in Yonkers. Over the next few years he would make every effort to acquire land northward along the river, via land grants from friendly British governors (he held a seat on the Governor's Council) or purchases from natives. By 1693, when reigning British monarchs William and Mary finally granted him a charter for Philipsburg Manor, he owned more than 50,000 acres.

But in 1682, that achievement was still ahead of him. His immediate task was to construct the milling and trading center on the Pocantico. A problem confronting him was where to find workers to build and run his mill and other operations. He soon found a solution—in the slave trade.

He also had to find tenants willing to clear fields and plant the all-important wheat crops. In his favor: New York City was now a busy grid of streets lined by tidy rows of buildings. Immigrants had begun to look beyond Manhattan for prime farmland. It helped that Indian attacks were no longer a real threat in the lower Hudson Valley. Settlers could live peaceably among the "heathen," their term for the unbaptized native Americans.

Philipse would make them an attractive offer: fertile land near the Hudson River, rent-free—at least for a while—in exchange for clearing the timber. Equally important for the Dutch settlers, who brought their Bibles with them from the old country, he'd take care of them.

He would find a place in the wilderness to build them a little church ...

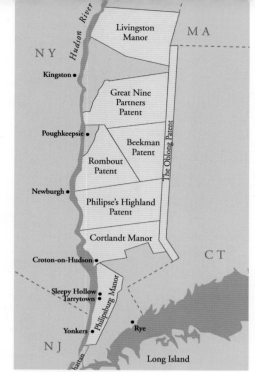

Manors Galore. A few wealthy landowners benefited from royal charters, or patents.
Map: Robert Romagnoli, Historic Hudson Valley.

The Land Barons

Royal patents concentrated land in the hands of a few wealthy owners in colonial New York. The patent granted to Frederick Philipse in 1693 ran from Spuyten Duyvil, at the tip of Manhattan, to the Croton River, in northern Westchester County, along twenty-two miles of Hudson riverfront. Philipse anticipated the increasing value of land near the river, used for transporting people and cargoes. Today the manor would be worth an astronomical sum— Westchester County commercial land may exceed $1 million per acre.

In all, Philipsburg Manor comprised more than 50,000 acres, nearly a fifth of the county. Even John D. Rockefeller's expansive 3,500-acre estate, which he bought in 1893 near Tarrytown, would be just a small island in the enormous tract owned by Frederick Philipse.

An Early Legend. Long before Irving wrote "The Legend of Sleepy Hollow," there was the legend of Cuffy's dream about the dam and the church.
Illustration: Currier & Ives; Historic Hudson Valley.

THE CHURCH'S BEGINNINGS

Bergen, N.J., Church, 1680. This octagonal design in rural Holland was also used in America.

A legend passed down over generations hints at what might have happened in 1685. According to the legend, after the dam for the gristmill at Upper Mills was finished, Frederick Philipse had his workers lay the church foundation on a knoll above the northern bank of the Pocantico, some 150 yards from the gristmill. But when the river flooded, the dam broke. Anxious to have his gristmill working—and receive its income—Philipse pulled his workers off the church project to repair the dam. Floods destroyed it yet again, and then a third time.

One day an enslaved African named Cuffy (other accounts refer to him as Harry), who worked at Philipsburg Manor, told Philipse about his recurring dream. In it, God told him that unless his master completed the church, the dam would not hold. "Finish the church," pleaded the slave, fearful of God's wrath.

Upon hearing him out, Philipse was uneasy, so the legend goes. The Dutch Reformed religion of the day, which he subscribed to, acknowledged omens as indicators of God's will. Now he had two omens—the floods and the message from the slave. He quickly sent his workers back to the church to finish building it.

And the dam held.

The legend about Cuffy and his dream may have arisen to account for the long delay between the start of construction in 1684 and the church's formal organization as Dutch Reformed in 1697. However, historians largely agree that construction was completed by 1685. The year is engraved on the church bell that was cast in Holland and installed in the belfry by Philipse's workers.

A more practical explanation for the long delay is the scarcity of ministers in the colony. Church authorities in the Netherlands oversaw religious matters in colonial Dutch Reformed churches to the smallest detail, hindering the rise of church leaders born in the colonies. Ministers received theological training and ordination in the Netherlands. By 1697, there were just seven Reformed Church ministers in America, and four of them spoke French. At the same time, twenty-six Dutch Reformed churches existed in the former New Netherland colony, most led by laymen. The Philipses wanted a minister. Where would he come from? In 1697 the answer came: Guiliam Bertholf of Hackensack, N.J. The consistory (board of elders and deacons) hired him as part-time minister. The church "did not owe its being to him, but he organized it," wrote Rev. David Cole, church historian.

Philipse, a former carpenter and building consultant, designed a church quite unlike the small octagonal churches the Dutch built in New Netherland in the seventeenth century. He gave the church a near-rectangular shape, with a three-sided apse at the east end and windowsills seven feet above the floor. At thirty-three feet wide by nearly fifty-eight feet long, it was larger than typical octagonal churches too.

In fact, Philipse's design bears a resemblance to a thirteenth-century church in Exmorra, Netherlands, near Bolsward, his birthplace. That church also has high sills, a low entrance and two weather vanes. Note Exmorra's steep-pitched roof. Such a roof may have been a feature of the manor church at one time, later replaced with the two-slope gambrel roof on the church today. (The gambrel was not popular in the Hudson Valley until the 1720s. That was when the steep-pitched roof on the Upper Mills manor house was replaced with a gambrel.)

Lookalike. Church in Exmorra, Holland, is similar to Old Dutch. Photo: C. R. Schriek.

Philipse chose fieldstone as his building material. It was a common choice among builders in the Hudson Valley. Enslaved Africans probably quarried, dressed, and loaded the stones on wagons for transport to the building site. Masons made an effort to match stones in size and shape, then mortared them into place using Hudson River mud mixed with straw; lime from oyster shells may have been added to make it more durable. Slender yellow bricks, brought from Holland, trimmed the windows and door. A sprightly belfry and two weather vanes finished off the roof.

The little church in the wilderness was now ready to welcome Frederick and Margaret Philipse, tenant farmers, enslaved Africans and native Americans.

Then and Now. At left is an artist's rendering of how the building looked when built. For the windows, the artist measured a pair of original shutters found in the belfry. The church (right) has not changed much over the years, though the door was moved and the windows enlarged. Illustration (left): David M. Clarke, 1963.

SLAVES AT THE OLD DUTCH?

The legend of the enslaved African whose dream spurred on Frederick Philipse to build the church reveals a surprise to some: slaves labored on Philipse's church and manor—and elsewhere in the colony.

In fact, race-based slavery took root early in New Netherland. Unable to attract enough workers to the colony, the Dutch West India Company brought in blacks from Africa and the West Indies as slave laborers in the early years. As the colony grew, so did the number of slaves. Slavery was legal in New York until 1827.

"Because the Dutch were deeply involved in the slave trade throughout the western hemisphere, there was, as might be expected, little criticism of slavery by the religious leaders in the Netherlands," wrote Gerald De Jong in *Church History* (1971), a publication of the American Society of Church History. Even churchmen who did criticize it focused their concern on the slaves' salvation, rather than on the inherent evil of slavery. At least one church even owned slaves. In 1770 the Dutch Reformed Church in New York City took an enslaved African valued at £45 in payment for back rent owed it. The minister, Rev. Johannes Ritzema, who was also part-time minister of the Philipsburg Manor church, signed the consistory document.

Philipse entered the slave trade in the 1680s while he was building Upper Mills. One of his first slave-trading ventures resulted in the unplanned arrival of enslaved Africans at the Mills, as recounted by historian Dennis Maika in "Encounters: Slavery and the Philipse Family, 1680–1751," published in *Dutch New York*:

> In 1685, Philipse's ship the Charles boarded 146 slaves from Soyo, a port on the Kongolese coast, and sailed to Barbados. Only 105 survived the voyage, 21 of whom were ill upon arrival. Nine of the infirm slaves were sent to New York, deemed "refuse cargo" unacceptable for sale in Barbados. Eight were delivered to Philipse's 19-year-old son Adolph near Rye, New York, who then took them approximately 15 miles across Westchester County to the confluence of the Hudson and Pocantico Rivers, where the Upper Mills was under construction. The ninth was sent to New York City, perhaps to serve in Philipse's Manhattan household.

This small group of enslaved Africans at Upper Mills was soon joined by others. They were put to work on the dam, the mill, the manor—and the church.

In 1702, Frederick Philipse owned about forty slaves, making him one of the largest slaveholders in the Hudson Valley.

Myth or Fact

Of Noble Birth?

An oft-repeated story about Frederick Philipse is that he descended from Bohemian nobility. For example, Westchester County historian Robert Bolton wrote in 1848 that Frederick's father "was the Hon. Viscount Felyps, of Bohemia, who sprang from the ancient Viscounts of that name and country."

Searches of archives in his birth village of Bolsward and elsewhere in the Netherlands point to more ordinary origins. Contrary to Bolton's assertion, Frederick Philipse's grandfather was a well-to-do tradesman from Leeuwarden, capital of Friesland province. He was named Douwe Filipsz and he sold herbs and spices on the main shopping street. Great-grandfather Philippus Douwesz (the family followed a patronymic naming convention) also lived in Leeuwarden; the family may have become members of the Reformed Church as early as 1581.

Whatever truth is in the old family story is lost to us today.

Middle Colonies. Matthew Seutter painted this ink-and-watercolor map in Germany between 1730–1740. It has an inset of early Manhattan and its Dutch-style architecture. Illustration: Historic Hudson Valley.

The Date Debate

Over the years, the congregation has celebrated 1697 as the date the church was officially organized. However, settlers would have begun meeting in 1685 at the newly built church for prayer and Bible study. The church's First Record Book, *created in 1715, says the early settlers "lived as real Christians among the heathen, deeming it right and necessary, on the Lord's day, to come together in a convenient place, and with each other to pray to God."*

The Philipse church may not have been the first one on the site. Earlier settlers who used the old gristmill Philipse had found may have met in an earlier building on the knoll, possibly of wood frame construction. When Philipse arrived, an existing graveyard there already had some fifty graves dating as far back as the 1640s.

A nineteenth-century stone plaque near the door created confusion about the church's origins. It states the church was "erected by Frederick Philips and Catharine Van Cortlandt his wife, 1699." In 1897, Edgar Mayhew Bacon,

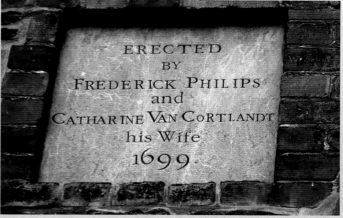

Is That So? Contrary to this inscription, the church was erected in 1685. It was organized as Dutch Reformed in 1697.

church historian, wrote in his Chronicles of Tarrytown and Sleepy Hollow *that the plaque, which is in English, must have been ordered and placed near the door when the door was moved to the west wall in 1837. The statement is inscribed in English, "a language not used in the church until sometime subsequent to the War for Independence." Down through the years, it has tripped up countless writers and historians.*

17

HOW THE CHURCH WAS BUILT
The building remains virtually unchanged over the years.

Belfry
The open belfry shelters the 1685 bronze bell, 15.5" wide by 12.5" high.

Weather Vane
The seventeenth-century pennant atop this weather vane (see p. 20) bears Frederick Philipse's registered brand mark.

Roof
A Flemish gambrel roof with flaring eaves gives it a bell shape. The church may have had a pitched roof originally.

1685 Bell
Philipse's first wife, Margaret, ordered the bronze bell from bell founder Gerhard Schimmel of Deventer, Holland. Fanciful figures parade around the bell in two bands. The upper one has cherubs in a leaf and fruit ornament; the lower has flying birds, acanthus and an owl. Engraved on it is the year 1685 and a scriptural verse in Latin. From Romans 8:31, it reads *"Si Deus pro nobis quis contra nos?"* (If God is for us, who can be against us?).

Walls
Workers built heavy fieldstone walls, 24"–30" thick, and used Hudson River mud mixed with straw to seal the joints; lime from oyster shells was added to make the mortar more durable.

Windows
Originally there were six square windows fitted with iron bars and wooden shutters. In 1837, the square windows were replaced with larger, Gothic-arched windows.

Door
Originally in the south wall and trimmed in yellow brick from Holland, the door was moved to the west wall in 1837. The work coincided with a rerouting of the Albany Post Road near the church.

Patchwork
Thin yellow bricks from Holland originally framed the door and windows. They were removed when the windows were replaced and later used to patch holes in the walls.

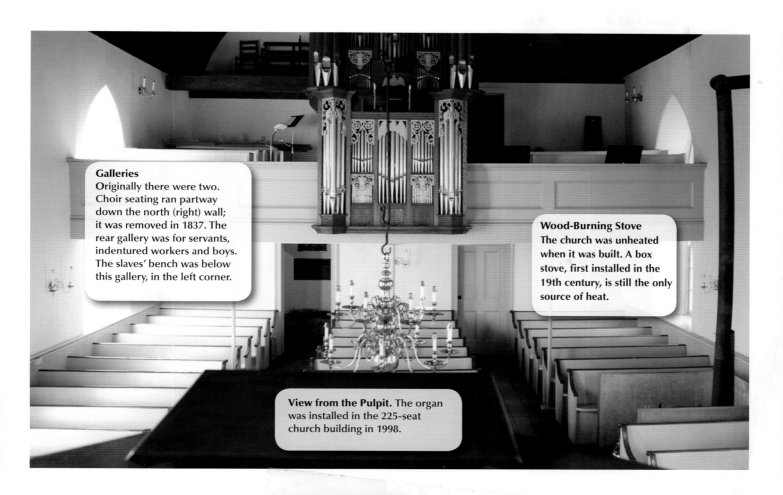

Galleries
Originally there were two. Choir seating ran partway down the north (right) wall; it was removed in 1837. The rear gallery was for servants, indentured workers and boys. The slaves' bench was below this gallery, in the left corner.

Wood-Burning Stove
The church was unheated when it was built. A box stove, first installed in the 19th century, is still the only source of heat.

View from the Pulpit. The organ was installed in the 225-seat church building in 1998.

Interior
The stone walls were originally whitewashed. As today, hand-hewn oak beams crossed the barrel ceiling to rest atop the side walls. The church was lit with candles, then and today.

"Thrones"
Seating for the Philipses was at either side of the pulpit, under the high-silled original windows. A canopy with drapes secured privacy. After the Revolution, the chairs were replaced with box seating for elders and deacons.

Pews
The first congregation sat on backless benches of hard oak. The present pews were installed in 1837.

Photo: Jesse Rinka Photography.

He Spelled It How?

" The weather vane still displays the monogram V.F., the initials of Vredry Flypse. As the first manor lord abandoned his early Dutch signature and adopted its English equivalent at a date earlier than that usually given for the building of the church, the initials V.F. must have also changed to F.F., or F.P."

Ever since Frederick Philipse died three centuries ago, visitors have puzzled over the initials on the wrought-iron pennant weather vane. The quote above, attributed to historian Edgar Mayhew Bacon a century ago, is still the common explanation.

But did Philipse ever spell his first name with a "V"? One Sleepy Hollow Restorations researcher in the 1970s found seventeen spellings of Philipse's name! Another searched the ancient records and concluded, "In the hundreds of times his name appears in the records, only once does either name begin with a 'V' and that is in a deposition written by a clerk in 1691. The name there is spelled 'Frederick Vlypson.'" Go figure.

Dutch Traders. An engraving of New Amsterdam circa 1643 shows traders who bring to mind Frederick and Margaret Philipse. Illustration: Historic Hudson Valley.

THE LADIES OF THE CHURCH: FREDERICK'S TWO WIVES

Margaret Hardenbroeck De Vries (1631 to about 1690): "Capable, but not attractive, and not very cultivated" was how Rev. John Knox Allen, D.D., writing in 1918, summed up Margaret Philipse, Frederick's first wife. She was a savvy businesswoman, though. She ran a shipping business between New Amsterdam and Europe. Solo.

She inherited the ships after the death of her first husband, Peter Rudolphus De Vries. Through twenty-five years of marriage to Frederick, whom she wed in 1662, she kept a close scrutiny over her ships, meanwhile sending their four children and Eva, the child from her first marriage, to Europe to be educated. We don't know what Margaret thought of her husband's new venture, but he surely sought her opinion. She had both family and business connections and was a valuable partner.

Tradition says Margaret made the trip upriver from their home in Manhattan to view the progress on the mill and the church. Elders referred to her in the church's *First Record Book* of 1715 as "Margaretta of blessed memory," which implies that she took an interest in the church. And why not? Both she and Frederick came from the same Reformed tradition as the pious Dutch settlers.

Margaret did not live long enough to see the arrival of the first *domine* (minister). She died about 1690. How or where she passed away, or even if her coffin is among sixteen or so in the family crypt beneath the church, is not known.

Catherine Van Cortlandt (1652–1730): Frederick was again lucky in love, marrying another wealthy widow, Catherine Van Cortlandt, then forty, twenty-five years younger than Philipse and the daughter of an influential family in New York City. Just a year after their marriage in 1692, the reigning monarchs, William and Mary, granted Philipse a patent for Philipsburg Manor. With it came handsome, if largely honorary, titles—lord and lady of Philipsburg Manor.

Lady Catherine was quite different from her predecessor. Rev. Allen described Catherine as "young, attractive, of sweet disposition, and of charming manners." She certainly charmed her husband's tenant farmers; they expressed their affection for her in the most flowery language—"a relic of the feudal age," wrote Rev. David Cole, who translated the *First Record Book* of 1715. In it she is described as "the Right Honourable, blessed, very wise, foreseeing Lady Catharina Phillips, widow of Lord Frederick Phillips of blessed memory who did in this locality, in the most praiseworthy manner, further the service of God."

Historian Robert Bolton relates a tradition that Catherine traveled to Upper Mills on horseback, riding pillion behind her brother Jacobus, to oversee the building of the church. This seems unlikely, since the church was completed before she and Frederick married. She acknowledged as much in her will, by referring to it as the church "built by my husband."

But she did take an active interest in the church in its early years. Rev. David Cole wrote that she spent "three or four years" searching for a minister. It must have helped to have the lord and lady of Philipsburg Manor behind the effort. Rev. Guiliam Bertholf of Hackensack agreed to travel to Philipsburg a few times a year to preach and conduct the sacraments. He was a full-time *domine* for the two villages of Hackensack and Aquackanonk, both in East Jersey, but also had several other churches under his care. To prepare for his arrival, Catherine furnished the church beautifully and simply.

Philipse & Capt. Kidd

By the mid-1690s, smuggling was common in New York. Merchant ships, their holds full of rum, gunpowder and arms, streamed out of New York to the pirate haven of Madagascar. There the wares were exchanged for pirated cargoes. Ships returned stuffed with East Indian goods and Arabian gold. The American coast was riddled with hiding places for the stolen merchandise.

When the crackdown came, a bold sea captain named William Kidd received a royal commission to hunt down the pirates. Some New York merchants saw opportunity in backing Kidd's venture, in exchange for a share of the profits from captured pirate booty.

But instead of attacking the buccaneers, Kidd joined them! He was captured, tried and hanged. Frederick Philipse and some other merchants were suspected of having known Kidd's real purposes and benefited financially. Philipse was never charged with smuggling. But in 1698 he left the Governor's Council, where he'd held a seat for twenty years, under a cloud of suspicion.

A boulder on the banks of the Hudson near Upper Mills, long rumored to be a meeting place between Kidd and Philipse, is still called Kidd's Rock.

Treasures of the Church

In all church matters, Lady Catherine was guided by the Synod of Dort, the series of ecclesiastical conferences in the sixteenth century that had established the liturgy, forms of worship and government of the Dutch Reformed Church. In her will, she referred to the church "erected and built ... according to the discipline of the Synod of Dort." Some Synod decisions reflecting theologian John Calvin's influence had implications for how churches were furnished. Specifically, Calvin opposed most paintings and sculpture in churches and musical-instrument accompaniment to psalm singing.

Pulpit

Attention should be on the preaching, Calvin said. So in Philipse's church, the pulpit was front and center. And what a pulpit! Brought from the Netherlands, it was a work of art in warm, rich hues of mahogany and oak, octagonal and on a pedestal. Pastors ascended to the platform on six curving oak stairs. A hexagonal sounding board projected the *domine's* voice. The rich detail was in sharp contrast to the plainness of the bare, whitewashed stone interior walls. The original pulpit was removed in 1837. The reproduction in the church today is modeled on the 1656 pulpit at First Church of Albany, believed to bear a close likeness to the original Philipsburg pulpit.

Communion Table

The Dutch draw-top table of oak with ebony inlay seen in the church today was donated by Frederick and Catherine Philipse. It was made between 1660 and 1680 in the Netherlands and given to the church sometime after 1692. The bulbous turned legs are typical Dutch style. The leaves extend the three-by-five-foot table to nine feet. In the early days, congregants would gather around it for Communion, slipping an offering under the tablecloth before returning to their seats. The church also owns two walnut eighteenth-century side chairs. One can imagine Lord and Lady Philipse in all their finery seated at the Communion table, and a bewigged Rev. Bertholf pouring the sacramental wine into their personal sterling-silver beakers. Lady Catherine bequeathed the table to the church, along with a damask tablecloth.

Photo at left: Jesse Rinka Photography.

Colonial Silver. The beakers and bowl, given to the church by the Philipses, are among the most treasured silver in American church collections.

Communion Beaker

Inscribed "Fredryck Flypse," this late-seventeenth-century silver beaker is 6.5 inches high and decorated with engraved interlacing bands of leaves and flowers. There is no maker's mark. According to *New York Silversmiths of the 17th Century*, published by the Museum of the City of New York, colonial silversmiths were hired to make the Communion silver for local Dutch churches. This beaker testifies to their skills. Frederick Philipse likely gave this beaker and the baptismal basin to the church before his death, as they are not mentioned in his will. The beaker is still used in Communion services.

Source: Appraisal, in church files.

Baptismal Basin

This 10.5-inch wide solid silver baptismal basin is late seventeenth century. It is inscribed "Fredryck Flypse" on the rim. The touchmark of the maker is thought to be that of Jurian Blanck Jr. or Jacob Boelen, silversmiths in New York City. The basin is still used by the church. The basin and Philipse's beaker were exhibited in 1932 at the Metropolitan Museum of Art. Later, in 1962, the Museum of the City of New York exhibited the silver.

Communion Beaker

This silver beaker was made in the late seventeenth century and has the marks of a Dutch silversmith. It is inscribed "Catharina Van Cortlant." It is nearly seven inches high and engraved with floral motifs and oval medallions symbolizing faith, hope and charity. A similar beaker, owned by First Church of Albany, is dated 1678 and was made by Ahasuerus Hendricks, the earliest silversmith in New York. Catherine bequeathed her beaker to the church and it is also in use.

END OF AN ERA

In 1700, Frederick wrote his will, perhaps motivated by the death in Barbados of his eldest son, Philip, and his wife, Maria Sparks. Philip and perhaps Maria succumbed to island fevers, which took a heavy toll on sugar plantation owners and slaves alike. Philipse sent a ship to fetch his grandson, the future lord of Philipsburg Manor.

Two years later, in December 1702, Frederick Philipse also died. His will divided the bulk of his estate among his surviving children and grandson. He bequeathed Upper Mills to son Adolph, thirty-seven. Upper Mills comprised the land north of Dobbs Ferry to the Croton River, including the church. Lower Mills, the mill and manor house in Yonkers, was set aside for seven-year-old Frederick II at his coming of age. Frederick entrusted his grandson's upbringing to Catherine.

Of the twenty-one slaves at Upper Mills, Philipse bequeathed fifteen to Adolph. Five went to Lower Mills. Philipse's will stipulated "the Negroe woman Old Susan shall dwell and continue on the plantation at the Upper Mills so long as she lives."

As for Frederick Philipse, the far-sighted merchant and entrepreneur—his body was entombed in the family crypt, beneath the floorboards of his little stone church, and it still lies there undisturbed.

“ THE CHURCH ITSELF WAS A MONUMENT OF BY-GONE DAYS.”

—WASHINGTON IRVING, “WOLFERT'S ROOST,” 1855

Upper Mills. The mill at Philipsburg Manor was painted by an unknown artist, circa 1850.
Illustration: Historic Hudson Valley.

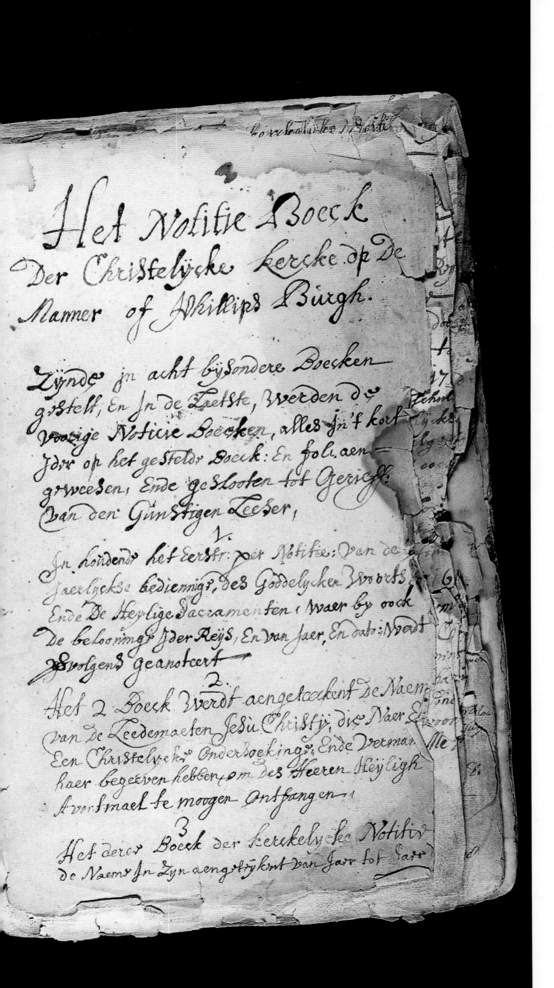

In 1697, the first church families eagerly awaited the arrival of their new pastor, Domine Guiliam Bertholf, who traveled several times a year from Hackensack, N.J., and was rowed across the choppy Hudson. What was a service in Dutch like? And what does the church's *First Record Book* tell us about the early settlers? Alas, in 1730, the church lost its great patroness. Lady Catherine Philipse passed away that year. The second pastor, Domine Johannes Ritzema, became embroiled in the church controversies of the day. Decades of prosperity followed—the calm before the storm.

A Gathering Place. The church, with its massive stone walls and spritely belfry, has been welcoming worshippers for well over 300 years.
Photo, previous page: First Record Book, 1715.

THE FIRST FAMILIES

Though it seems small and quaint today, Frederick Philipse's church was an impressive structure in the eyes of seventeenth-century pioneers. Its sturdy walls were skillfully constructed of stone, the windows framed with imported yellow brick. The sanctuary displayed furnishings made of polished mahogany and oak … and even fine silver. An engraved bronze bell from Holland, set in a lofty belfry, called the devout settlers to worship.

In comparison, those early settlers built crude cabins for themselves. They poured their strength into clearing fields for planting. Hardship and privation, loneliness and often danger filled their days. Household belongings were modest, mostly what they made themselves, down to the utensils. Their food stores had to sustain them over a long winter, and often ran very low by spring. Going to church meant traveling over primitive trails made by natives long before the Europeans arrived. One such trail ran northward from Manhattan along the east side of the Hudson River, passing close by the church.

It is unknown if the few fur traders, fishermen and farmers who arrived as early as the 1640s remained in the area, but quite possibly they had moved on before Philipse bought the Pocantico River Valley in 1681. Philipse's tenants—the first recorded settlers—were primarily Dutch who arrived in the 1680s and 1690s. Some set out for Upper Mills as soon as they got off the ship from the Netherlands, but most had been in the colony awhile, living in Dutch communities in Lange Eylandt (Long Island) and Breuckelen (Brooklyn), biding their time until they could afford to buy farmland.

Among them were a few French-speaking Protestants who'd fled Catholic persecution in their native countries. The French Protestants were called Huguenots and French-speaking Belgian Protestants were Walloons. Both initially found refuge in the Netherlands before immigrating to America. By 1697, there were about twenty poor families living on Philipsburg Manor.

"IT WAS HERE BEFORE THERE WAS A UNITED STATES OF AMERICA, BEFORE THERE WAS A NEW YORK STATE, OR A COUNTY OF WESTCHESTER. IT WAS HERE WHEN THIS TERRITORY WAS STILL A PART OF THE NEW WORLD. IT MIGHT WELL BE SAID OF THIS CHURCH AS MOSES SAID OF ISRAEL: 'HE FOUND HIM IN A DESERT LAND, AND IN THE HOWLING WASTE OF A WILDERNESS HE ENCIRCLED HIM, HE CARED FOR HIM, HE KEPT HIM AS THE APPLE OF HIS EYE.'"

—REV. WILLIAM R. BUITENDORP, PASTOR, FIRST REFORMED CHURCH OF NORTH TARRYTOWN, 1952–1970

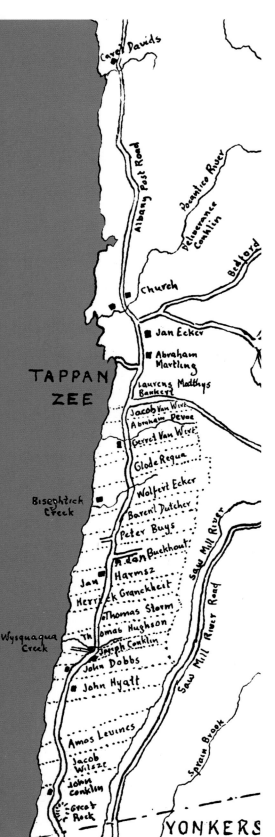

Map labels (top to bottom):
Cave David's
Albany Post Road
Pocantico River
Perseverance Conklin
Bedford
Church
Jan Ecker
Abraham Martling
TAPPAN ZEE
Laurens Mathys Bankert
Jacob Van Wirk
Abraham Devoe
Gerret Van Wirk
Glode Requa
Wolfert Ecker
Bisenhtick Creek
Barent Dutcher
Peter Buys
Jan Buckhout
Jan Harmsz
Merry
k Granckheit
Thomas Storm
Thomas Hughson
Wysquaqua Creek
Joseph Conklin
John Dobbs
John Hyatt
Saw Mill River
Saw Mill River Road
Sprown Brook
Amos Levines
Jacob Wiltze
John Conklin
Great Rock
YONKERS

Who Lived Where? Dutch, Huguenot and Walloon farmers lived along the river.
Map: Westchester County Historical Society.

THE SETTLERS

Among the families who lived on Philipsburg Manor in 1697, when the church on Philipsburg Manor was formally organized as Dutch Reformed, are these:

Joachim Van Wert (or Wouters**)** was born around 1637, possibly in Long Island. Frederick Philipse may have brought him from Midwout (Flatbush) about 1683 to run the mill. He and his wife, Christine Jans, had eight children. Joachim and Christine were listed as the sixth and seventh members on the first member list of the manor church. Van Wert was an elder.

Laurens Mathys Bankert, who was born about 1658, came from the same part of Long Island as Van Wert. He may have been brought to the area in the spring of 1682 by Frederick Philipse to look after his affairs at Upper Mills. "It is not unlikely that they [Van Wert and Bankert] shared the honors as the earliest recorded settlers of Tarrytown," wrote historian Grenville Mackenzie. To Bankert and his wife, Jannetje Hendricks, went the honor of having Lady Catherine Philipse as a witness at their child's baptism in 1701. It is the only time, according to church records, that she took part in a baptism at the manor church. The child's name, Adolph, was not common on the baptism register. Might he have been named after Catherine's stepson, Adolph Philipse, who would inherit Upper Mills the following year?

Wolfert and Jan Ecker brought their families to the Tarrytown area about 1691. Wolfert, who was born about 1668 in Flatbush, was the patriarch of the Eckers, or Ackers, in the area. The brothers were the first two deacons of the manor church. Jan, two years younger, was even authorized to conduct funerals. Wolfert built his house by the river a few miles south of the mills. Washington Irving would later write a fanciful story called "Wolfert's Roost" about the settler, and buy his homestead (for more about Irving, see chapter 6).

Among the immigrants who arrived directly from the Netherlands, without first settling in Long Island, was **Abraham De Revier**, a name that suggests a Walloon origin. He brought his wife and sons to Philipsburg after emigrating from South Holland sometime before 1697. De Revier was a man of some importance in the church. He was the first elder, and his name stands second on the member roll after Lady Catherine Philipse. The Old Dutch Church owes its earliest records to his habit of taking private notes. No official records were kept until 1715, when the consistory asked church member Dirck Storm, known for his fine handwriting, to create records dating back to 1697. Storm relied heavily on De Revier's private memoranda.

Dirck Storm was a man of letters who had tried a variety of jobs since immigrating to the colony in 1662 with his family from Osch, North Brabant, in Holland. He

Philipsburg Manor Farmer. Today Frederick Philipse's Upper Mills is a living-history museum near the old manor church. Photo: Historic Hudson Valley.

had been town clerk in Breuckelen, then tried his hand at real estate, teaching, tavern-keeping, and farming. In 1696 he was a tax collector for Westchester County. Storm later moved to Tappan, N.Y., where he was a *voorleser*, or lay clergyman, at its Dutch church. He arrived at Philipsburg in 1704 and began attending the manor church.

It's a good thing he came. Storm would play an important role in the church. In 1715, the elders and deacons sought to make amends for not keeping minutes or maintaining public registers of members, baptisms and marriages. They commissioned Storm to make, as he described it, "a written record of what has already passed, as full a one as we can find out that is in strict accord with the facts." The resulting *Het Notitie Boeck*, or the *First Record Book*, is one of the most treasured possessions of the Reformed Church of the Tarrytowns, which now oversees the Old Dutch Church, and a priceless document of the early colonial period.

Writing about Philipsburg Manor without mentioning the **Van Tassel** (variant spellings: Van Texel, Van Tessel) family would be like leaving Shakespeare's Hamlet out of the play, as one descendant noted on the family website. Although the name is no longer ubiquitous around Tarrytown, Van Tassels were prominent in the church for many generations. The name originally meant "from Texel," an island in the North Sea off the Dutch coast.

Cornelis Jansen Van Tassel, born about 1600, was an early settler on Long Island. He married Catoneras, the daughter of Indian chief Wyandice, *sachem* of the Montauk Indians of the north shore. Their son, Jan Cornelis Van Tassel, a deacon and an elder at the church, and his wife, Antje, settled just north of Philipsburg

Family Names

Family names of Dutch, Huguenot and Walloon origin are well represented in the church registers. In time, names typical of English, German and other cultures were added. Here is a sampling of the families of Philipsburg:

Dutch *Van Wart, Ecker, See, Paulding, Van Tassel, Storm, Buckholt, Martling, Lent, Young, Aertse*

Huguenots *(from France): Devoe, Sie, Requa, Boule, Foseur*

Walloons *(from Belgium): Delancy, Delameter, De Revier, Gardenier, Guiliamse, Mabie*

English *Underhill, Lawrence, Odell, Tompkins, Chatterton, Rossel, Pugsley, Archer, Honeywell, Barnes*

Germans *(arriving from 1720–40): Hileker, Koel, Syffer, Montross, and Romer from Switzerland*

Philipsburg Rents

The first settlers lived on the land rent-free. Later, when they paid rent, they had no written leases. Tenants were required to bring their grain and cut timber to Philipse's gristmill and sawmill. They owned outright any buildings put on the land, and they had the right to pass their leases on to their children. They could even sell their leases, though Philipse received part of the sale price.

Rents were collected on annual "rent days," when the lord of the manor feasted his tenantry in royal fashion. The rent varied from a minimum of two fat hens or a day's work upward.

In the early days, rents were "known by the name of Tithe, which was a rent payable not always in the proportion of one-tenth of the annual produce, but diversely," wrote a clerk named John Anstey, in 1786. John Davids was living on his father Carel Davids's farm in 1760. His rent: six pounds, four shillings and sixpence. In A Land of Peace: The Early History of Sparta, *writer Philip Field Horne estimates that was equal to about forty-one days of wages for a farm laborer.*

about 1684. His nine children were baptized there. Three of his sons, Jacob, Jan and Cornelis, settled in Philipsburg, thus ensuring the Van Tassel name would be well represented in church history and the local Revolutionary War history. Washington Irving was so captivated by the Van Tassels and their stories and heroics that he drew upon humorous snippets of their history when creating his enchanting, albeit fictitious stories, including "The Legend of Sleepy Hollow."

Also well represented in church and Revolutionary War history is the **Martling family** (variant spellings: Martlenghs, Martlings). The first Abraham Martling on the manor was born in Staten Island in 1693. He probably settled in present-day Tarrytown as a young man of twenty-one; he joined the church in 1716, the last new member to be recorded by Dirck Storm. His house was at the intersection of present-day Hamilton Place and Route 9 (Broadway). It became the Van Tassel Tavern in the Revolution. Martling was a pillar of the church, serving as both deacon and later elder, as well as a blacksmith, justice of the peace and first recorded town clerk of Philipsburg. He had many descendants through his nine children. He lived until 1761. His headstone, located behind the church, is one of the oldest in the churchyard. The inscription is in Dutch.

Matthys Janszen Buckhout was a sea captain who probably settled in Yonkers first and later moved to the vicinity. His son Captain John (or Jan) Buckhout, born about 1682, was the patriarch of one of the largest families in the manor church, in terms of offspring. A farmer in what is now Irvington, John, a veteran of the French and Indian War, married Mary Bankert in 1710, and they had seventeen children, of whom thirteen survived. He was married again in 1753, to a widow with young children, whom he also brought up. His gravestone says that when he passed away in 1785, age 103, he "left behind him when he died 240 children and grandchildren." We can only speculate: if the gravestone is accurate, Buckhout's offspring must have averaged seventeen children each. Or perhaps the count included great-grandchildren as well!

Carel Davids was a French Huguenot born in Canada, the son of a fur trader who moved his family from Montreal to Kingston, N.Y., in 1682. Carel was living on the manor by 1698. He married Antje Van Lent at the church, and they raised eleven children. Prominent descendant William Davids lived on a hill east of the church that was visited by George Washington in Revolutionary times.

Pewter Plate. This plate bears the initials of Esther and Isaac Sie, whose names appear on the first member register of the church. The plate bears the marks of English pewterer Richard Goeing, who worked 1735–1766.

THE FIRST WORSHIP SERVICE

Dutch parents loved to date a child's life from his or her baptism. In fact, church records rarely mention the actual birth date of a child. One can only imagine the joy and excitement when the settlers learned that Lady Catherine's search for a minister had succeeded, and **Domine Guiliam Bertholf** would soon arrive to preach and conduct the sacraments. There would be baptisms! The families marked the date: Sunday, April 21, 1697, two weeks after Easter.

Nearly all of the Philipsburg settlers turned out for this happy occasion. And why not? It was a rare chance to leave their isolated farms and find out how other families had fared over the winter. The *domine* would bring news of friends and family in distant settlements in New York and New Jersey, where he supervised a half-dozen or more other congregations. The snow and ice had melted. New shoots were popping up, and families could see a slight shimmer of green in the woods. It lifted their spirits.

So, early on April 21, men hitched horse to wagon and the whole family climbed in, all dressed in their best clothes. The *vrouw* (wife) wrapped the children warmly and tucked them in for the long ride. Young people set off ahead, impatient for the day's adventures.

Outside the church, a bench stood between the door and the middle window. That's where people rested while awaiting the *domine*.

What a colorful display of finery came their way! There was old Lord Philipse, now seventy, and Lady Catherine, twenty-five years his junior, with family and guests, all elegantly dressed. "The women wore short gowns of rich brocade or stiff silk, quilted and padded, and cut short to show the neat ankles in their red, clocked stockings," wrote church historian Edgar Mayhew Bacon in his 1897 book, *Chronicles of Tarrytown and Sleepy Hollow.*

"The men flourished in long, skirted blue coats, with buttons of silver and gold, over silken hose. Their wigs and buckles showed that neither head nor feet were considered beyond the pale of adornment. The children were miniature parodies on their elders; and the *domine* appeared in his suit of respectable black.

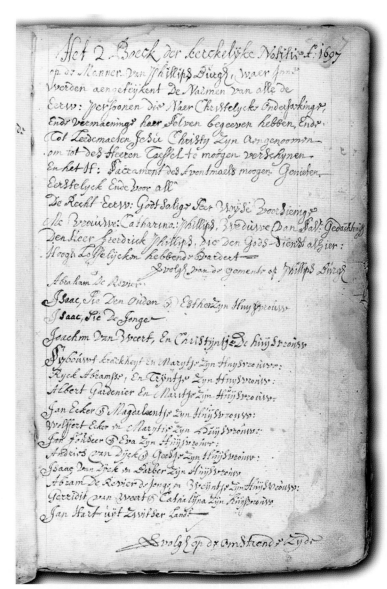

First Member Register of 1715. The first page of the member list is headed by Lady Catherine Philipse.

Tinkling Bell.
A bell attached to a small cloth bag used for collections gave notice when a coin was dropped in.

Myth or Fact

Did Enslaved Africans Join the Church?

In the early eighteenth century, Reformed churches in New York generally did not allow enslaved Africans to become members. If the manor church followed the Tappan Reformed Church, also organized by Rev. Guiliam Bertholf, enslaved persons were generally forbidden Communion and marriage ceremonies performed by a minister. The custom was for a slave to attend his master's church. By tradition, at least some of the twenty or so slaves at Upper Mills at that time worshipped in the church.

No slave names appear to be recorded in the Old Dutch's early member lists or marriage registry. One enslaved woman, however, is among the early listings in the baptism register. Susanna Derckse, identified as a Negro woman belonging to John Harmse, was baptized on March 29, 1729. Harmse was an elder of the church in 1715–16.

"Next were the farmers, dressed in homespun, linsey-woolsey, and all manner of durable stuffs, the girls trying humbly to imitate the splendors of the great dames," continued Bacon. "After the farmer folk came the Negro slaves, and the poorer white hangers-on of the place and the aboriginal landowners."

Inside the church the settlers' eyes adjusted to the reduced light that came through the high-silled, barred windows, the heavy shutters thrown open for the occasion. The soft light illumined the richly polished wood of the octagonal mahogany pulpit and sounding board. The Philipses seated themselves in their cushioned and curtained box seats, like thrones, one on either side of the pulpit. It was a custom from ancient feudal days, but at the time "men had not yet begun to be born free and equal," as Bacon wrote. In another generation or two, people would come to resent the extravagant display of privilege and tear out the thrones.

But for now the lord and lady of the manor reposed in splendid privacy and comfort. As for the farmers, they crowded onto backless oak benches. Presumably, with their stronger backs, they could stand the strain of the hours-long service better than their patrons.

The choir took their seats in a shallow gallery that ran along the north wall. In the west gallery, shallower than today, were the humble retainers and indentured servants, seated with the boys who were kept in order by the choir leader. Enslaved Africans sat below the gallery on a bench positioned near the door.

As to the service, a lay reader began worship with a Bible reading, followed by a psalm. One line at a time was read out loud by Jan Ecker, deacon, and then sung by the congregation. Without an organ, the singing was by ear and very uncertain. Some psalms took a half-hour to get through in this way, and all the while the congregation was standing. Washington Irving would later skewer the poor choirmasters who so laboriously struggled with the unmusical singing. In his story, "The Legend of Sleepy Hollow," the "singing master of the neighborhood," Ichabod Crane, took great pride in his station in front of the church gallery, where "in his own mind, he completely carried away the palm from the parson."

In the typical fashion of the day, Domine Bertholf entered the church after the choir began singing, knelt at the chancel to pray silently, then took the six stairs to the pedestal pulpit. From that lofty height, he read the Ten Commandments. After a prayer came a liturgical confession of sin and the reciting of the Apostles' Creed, followed by a lengthy sermon and a free-form prayer spoken from the heart. Domine Bertholf left behind no written sermons, but certainly would have taken them from the *Staten-Bijbel*, or the official States Bible. This first Dutch translation was approved by the Great Synod of Dort in 1618–19. As historian Firth Haring Fabend wrote in her book *A Dutch Family in the Middle Colonies, 1660–1800*, "Scarcely a Dutch home was without a copy."

Sometime during the worship service, a deacon passed around a small cloth bag attached to a long pole. These *sacjes*, as they were called, usually had a little bell hidden in the bottom or attached to a tassel, which tinkled when a coin was added. On Communion Sundays there was a second collection. For the Holy Sacrament, the Dutch table—the same one still to be seen in the church today—was drawn out to its full nine-foot length. Small groups came up to sit around it. The minister made an address to each group. Before they left the table, the people lifted the edge of the cloth and deposited under it sixpence or another sum, which was to be used only for the purchase of bread and wine for the sacrament.

At midday there was a break. Domine Bertholf joined the Philipses for lunch at the nearby manor house. With its attic storehouse, cellar kitchen and four rooms on two floors, the stone house was not grand—unless one compared it to the tenants' homes—but the Philipses had furnished it with the finest imported furniture and textiles. The draw-top table with its bulbous legs, very similar to the Communion table at the church, was set with snowy table linens, polished pewter plates and silver utensils and chafing dishes, and loaded down with every kind of food produced in the new homeland—game and fish and corn, pumpkins and squash among them.

Meanwhile, on the church grounds, the farmers and their families ate the lunch they had brought with them, and possibly gossiped a little. Young men and women looked after the horses that were tied up in a grove of locust trees along the mill-pond. A little innocent flirting doubtless went on in that grove, too, despite the *domine*'s solemn sermon in the morning about the vanity of all things here below.

Again, Irving pictures the scene in his "Legend of Sleepy Hollow" as schoolmaster Ichabod Crane attends service:

> *Our man of letters was peculiarly happy in the smiles of all the country damsels. How he would figure among them in the churchyard between services on Sundays! Gathering grapes for them from the wild vines that overran the surrounding trees; reciting for their amusement all the epitaphs on the tombstones; or sauntering, with a whole bevy of them, along the banks of the adjacent mill-pond; while the more bashful country bumpkins hung sheepishly back, envying his superior eloquence and address.*

A deacon taught Bible lessons to the young children or quizzed them on the morning sermon. In fact, schoolmaster was one of the many duties of the *voorleser*, the lay clergyman who led worship services in between visits from Domine Bertholf. The *domine* had been a schoolmaster himself in New Jersey

"IT IS DIFFICULT FOR US TO THINK OF THIS SIMPLE-HEARTED, PIOUS MAN [DOMINE BERTHOLF] FEELING ANY INTEREST IN THE ELEVATED AND CURTAINED PERCHES AT THE SIDE OF HIS PULPIT, PLACED FOR THE PURPOSE OF LIFTING SOME OF HIS HEARERS ABOVE OTHERS IN A HOUSE EXPRESSLY PLANNED OF GOD TO BRING RICH AND POOR, HIGH AND LOW, TOGETHER, AND EMPHASIZE THE FACT THAT GOD WAS THE MAKER OF THEM ALL. "THE GOOD DOMINE SIMPLY BORE THIS AS INSEPARABLE FROM THE TIMES, AND AS SOMETHING THAT HE COULD NOT CHANGE; THAT HIS HEART AND MIND WERE INFINITELY ABOVE IT, AND THAT HIS PREACHING WAS DIRECT AND FAITHFUL TO ALL ALIKE."

—REV. DAVID COLE, 1897

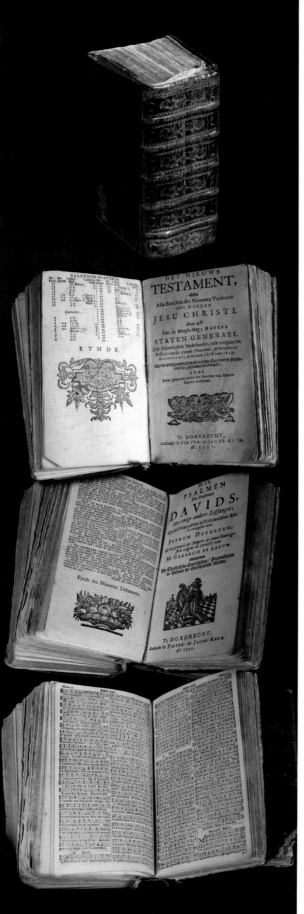

1731 Bible. This small Dutch Bible, one of the oldest in the church's collection, includes a section on Psalms set to music (bottom two photos).

before he became a minister. Teaching children the Heidelberg Catechism, the 1563 statement of faith adopted by the Dutch church, was still one of his duties; it was often the only schooling children got. "What is thine only comfort in life and in death?" he would begin. Their answer: "That I, with body and soul, both in life and death, am not my own but belong to my faithful Saviour Jesus Christ, who with his precious blood hath fully satisfied for all my sins and delivered me."

On that Sunday of April 21, when it came time for the baptisms, parents were called to the railing at the chancel. Twelve children were presented for baptism. Twenty-two parents (one couple, the De Witts, presented two boys, perhaps twins, named Paulus and Petrus) and twenty-two witnesses took part. Their names were later recorded in the *First Record Book*. The eighteen families named include Van Tassels, De Reviers, Davidses, Eckers, Abramses, Abramzens, Herricksens, Heyerts, De Witts, Lourenses, Springsteens, Giljons, Quoris, Jansens, Fausees, Storms, Van Werts and Krankheyts. This at a time when only twenty families lived on the manor!

Quite possibly the silver baptismal bowl that is still in the possession of the Reformed Church in Tarrytown made its debut at this time. One of the early colonial treasures of this country, the bowl has Frederick Philipse's name engraved on the rim. It was a gift to the church from the Philipses, perhaps presented on this day in honor of the first baptisms. This first service was made even more special by the fact that it was a Sunday service. Future visits by Domine Bertholf were to be on weekdays. He had agreed with Lady Catherine to return several times a year to preach and celebrate the sacraments, but he had congregations in Hackensack and Passaic, N.J. He arranged his schedule so he'd be home on Sunday to preach at those churches.

On future visits when Domine Bertholf visited Philipsburg, he would meet Theunis Van Houten, a member of his Tappan, N.Y., congregation, on a Monday and travel to the manor, rowing across the Hudson River at Sneden's Landing, in present-day Palisades. As soon as convenient, the congregation would assemble. He would baptize children born since his last visit. The next day he'd preach a sermon and conduct the Lord's Supper. He'd catechize children and visit the sick. Van Houten would take him back home, where he'd arrive in time to prepare for Sunday services. Then he'd set off the next day visiting other distant congregations.

Crossing the Hudson River definitely added an element of danger to Domine Bertholf's trips to Philipsburg. The river was strongly tidal, with fast currents and a deep channel. As historian Fabend wrote, "That such a perilous passage was taken, particularly in a rowboat, is striking testimony to the people's thirst for religion and Bertholf's determination to satisfy it."

THE FIRST MINISTER

The congregation liked their new *domine*, Guiliam Bertholf. Perhaps they felt he was one of them. The son of a wine merchant in Sluis, in the Dutch province of Zeeland, he had learned coopering, or barrel-making, in his youth. Upon arriving in the colonies in 1684, he took up the trade of baker, but his passion was to serve God. He was a *voorleser*, or lay clergy, in East Jersey for several years. He was ordained as a minister just three years before he became the pastor at Philipsburg.

PASTORS . A.D	
G.BARTHOLFF.	1697
J.RITZEMA .	1760
S.V.VOORHEES.	1785
J.F.JACKSON.	1795
T.G.SMITH .	1798
G.DUBOIS .	1838
J.WILSON .	1845
J.M.FERRIS .	1849
A.T.STEWART.	1852

Not Quite. This list of ministers in the church entry has the right names, though not necessarily the right spellings or even dates.

Given the scarcity of ministers, many wilderness congregations were eager for his help. As *voorleser* his duties included leading worship services in the absence of a minister, visiting the sick, and reading set sermons and printed prayers. Only ordained clergymen were allowed to preach their own sermons and conduct the sacraments. Congregations often grew close to their hardworking *voorleser*, preferring him to the Amsterdam-ordained ministers who came out from the city periodically to perform the sacraments.

Guiliam Bertholf was suspect to those ministers almost as soon as he arrived in the colony. Bertholf had been a disciple of a famous Pietist theologian in his home church in Zeeland, the heartland of Dutch Pietism. Pietists disdained what they called the "stiff-necked, rigid orthodoxy" of the mother church in Amsterdam, and its ministers who "chatter to the Lord in a cold voice," in the words of one eighteenth-century Pietist. Pietists believed such ministers lulled congregants into believing they could be saved by merely repeating rote prayers. Adherents of Pietism annoyed church authorities in Amsterdam by insisting on the need for a personal conversion experience to truly be saved.

Not long after Bertholf's arrival in America, a New York minister wrote to church authorities in Amsterdam:

> *Certain men came over last year with certificates from Sluis.... They were only tailors or shoemakers or cobblers, yet they endeavored to be promoted in this place or in that to the office of precentor [choirmaster] and schoolmaster. Some of them were assisted by me because of their great zeal, but how is it possible to agree with most of them? They speak against the church, public prayer and the liturgy.*

> " ALMOST AS IMPORTANT AS THE DOMINE WAS THE VOORLESER, WHO ALMOST GENERALLY WAS ALSO THE BELL RINGER, SEXTON, GRAVE DIGGER, FUNERAL INVITER, SCHOOLMASTER AND, SOMETIMES, TOWN CLERK."
>
> — ALICE MORSE EARLE, *HOME LIFE IN COLONIAL DAYS*, 1898

Tappan Zee. An early view of the Hudson River by Thomas Addis Emmet (1828–1919).

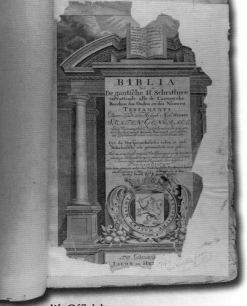

It's Official.
Every Dutch home
had this approved translation.
This Bible, from the Old Dutch
collection, dates to 1744.

In 1692, a minister from Albany and two from New York City jointly sent a letter of complaint to church authorities in Amsterdam. Several churches—principally those associated with Bertholf at one time or another—had turned against them. "The churches of Bergen, Hackensack, Staten Island and Harlem have deserted us, yielding to the power of evil," their letter said. "They say they can live well enough without ministers or sacraments."

The next year, Bertholf's Hackensack and Passaic congregations sent him to the Netherlands to be ordained. However, instead of applying to the Classis of Amsterdam, which supervised the churches in America, Bertholf went to Middelburg in Zeeland and was quickly ordained by the Classis of Walcheren. Upon his return in 1694, he accepted the invitation of the two churches to become their minister. As the sole New Jersey minister, he also agreed over time to organize and minister to at least nine other churches. The "Itinerating Apostle of New Jersey," as he has been called, kept a hectic schedule.

The Philipsburg congregation felt blessed to be one of the churches he supervised. The *First Record Book* of 1715 refers to the "learned and pious Domine Bertholf," along with this entry: "We hope and wish that our Almighty and Merciful God will permit this arrangement to continue yet for a long time." Indeed, Domine Bertholf ended up supervising the Philipsburg church for twenty-seven years.

History looks back on Guiliam Bertholf as one of the most valuable members of the denomination. As Fabend wrote, "Independent and adventurous on the one hand, he seemed to have valued harmony, tolerance, cooperation, and order." Rev. David Cole, *First Record Book* translator, describes him as "a man of profound spirituality, warm heart, great capacity for teaching." The manor church thrived under his guidance, which lasted until 1724. A Bertholf family history gives us these lasting words:

> *So godly was his life, so kindly his spirit, and with so much tact and prudence did he manage, that his influence still lives, and to this day a blessing seems to rest upon the churches that owe their formation to him, for they continue strong and shining lights in the denomination.*

THE CHURCH LOSES ITS PATRONESS

Since they lived in the city, the lord and lady of the manor attended church there most of the time, visiting the church at Philipsburg infrequently, mainly when the minister visited. Only Lady Catherine actually joined the Philipsburg church. There's little evidence Philipse took much interest in religion beyond what was required of a respectable man of the day. A churchman of a later generation put it this way, "Although he built the church, we are unable to find that he was altogether saintly."

Lady Catherine was its great benefactor, helping to furnish the church and arranging for Domine Bertholf to be the first minister. The congregation may not have seen much of her after 1702, when her husband died. Frederick bequeathed Upper Mills, including the church, to his son Adolph, thirty-seven, and Lower Mills, his gristmill and manor house in Yonkers, to his orphaned grandson, seven, also named Frederick. Lord Philipse's will charged Lady Catherine with overseeing the education of young Frederick. She took him to England and may have stayed there with him for several years. Eventually Frederick II married Joanna Brockholls, daughter of New York lieutenant governor Anthony Brockholls, and they settled into the manor house at Lower Mills. Catherine may have returned to her house in the city.

The church learned of her death in 1730 with great sorrow. But she did not forget the little Dutch church on Philipsburg Manor. In the quaintly written language of the day, she wrote in her will:

> I bequeath unto my Son in Law Adolph Philipse Esq. & to his heirs for Ever a Large Silver Beeker on which my name is Engraven, a Damaske Table Cloth five Ells and three quarters long and two an half broad with a Long Table In Trust to and for the Congregation of the Dutch Church Erected and Built at Phillipseburgh by my late Husband Frederick Philipse deced, according to the discipline of the Synod of Dort ... for the use of the Said Church and Congregation and to and for no other use and purpose whatsoever.

Catherine's body was laid to rest near her husband in the family crypt beneath the Philipsburg church. Her influence, however, lived on. In the baptism register for several years afterward, what was a very common girl's name? Yes, it was Catherine.

Wintry Chill

Travel was difficult over snow-blocked roads or river ice, and when the half-frozen families finally did arrive at church, it wasn't warm inside. The church was unheated! On cold days, the women and children carried fireproof containers that held hot coals (see below). Some of the men carried muffs. Still, the chill of the damp building must have been hard to bear. At the noon break, the congregation warmed up at a great fire built of logs. To the west of the church, where the road now runs, was at one time a shed with horse stalls at one end. Perhaps the congregation also built a heated "noon-house" with a chimney.

The First Record Book, 1715

The three-century-old *Het Notitie Boeck der Christentycke Kerck op de Manner op Philipsburgh*, or *the First Record Book of the Christian Church on Philipsburg Manor* (at top left: cover and first page), is one of the most important documents of the colonial church in America. The book was written in Dutch—the language spoken at the church until after the American Revolution—by church member Dirck Storm. Inside its fragile covers are a brief history of the church's origins, a few financial accounts of the early church, and four church registers: Members, Elders and Deacons, Marriages, and Baptisms. These begin in 1697 and continue until the Revolution. Despite Storm's initial effort to create church minutes, neither he nor any other clerk followed up—no minutes were kept through most of the eighteenth century.

Storm's handwriting disappears from the book after his last entry in May 1716. Other clerks continued the registers. Some "did pretty well," wrote Rev. David Cole, who translated the book. Others were "shockingly illiterate and blundering." During the Revolution, records become chaotic or stop altogether.

The *First Record Book* was already in bad shape by the beginning of the twentieth century, when Rev. Cole began his great work of translation. Several leaves had broken from their stitching, and a few pages were badly rotted on their edges. "In a few cases words have been carried away," he wrote. "No doubt even a few dates have been lost." Today the old book belongs to the Reformed Church of the Tarrytowns, which continues the congregation of the Old Dutch Church of Sleepy Hollow. The fragile book is rarely displayed.

The Member Register (pictured left, third from top). Dirck Storm in his "full, round, clear handwriting," wrote Cole, recorded the names of the earliest members of the manor church. With just seventy-five names from 1697 to 1715, it is likely that Storm named only those persons still living in 1715, according to Cole. The member register in the *First Record Book* ends in 1775.

The Elders and Deacons Register (left, bottom). Beginning in 1697 and ending in 1776, the consistory register has a single addition in 1790.

The Marriage Register. The banns—legal notices of intended marriages—were often posted somewhere inside colonial churches, or nailed to the door, but weddings usually took place at the bride's parents' home. Justices of the peace could legally conduct weddings under the early Dutch and later British governments. Marriage registrations were recorded in the *First Record Book* until 1790. The register falls into disarray during the Revolution, with missing dates and details.

The Baptism Register. Baptisms take place annually until 1702, then a few times a year until 1778. During the period of the Revolution and later, the record is jumbled. A final few fragments are dated 1791. It almost always omits birth dates.

Preface for the Kind Reader

In creating the *First Record Book,* church member Dirck Storm starts with a "Preface for the Kind Reader," in which he gives a brief history of how the church came into being. An excerpt:

After Lord Frederick Philipse had bought and come into possession of the land tract, he contracted with a number of people to come and live upon it without charge that the land might quickly be put to use and settled.

And then further this record is made to testify with what kindly feeling these early Christian settlers conducted themselves amid the heathendom of the region, and lived as real Christians among the heathen, deeming it right and necessary on the Lord's Day, to come together at a convenient place, and with each other to pray to God with their whole hearts.

And next we put on record that these people thought it imperative to look for

a Reformed Church minister, willing to preach and administer the sacraments for them three or four times a year, that the congregation might thereby be, by the grace of God, benefited through the communion ("the bonds") of His Holy Sacraments, after the usage of the Christian Reformed Religion.

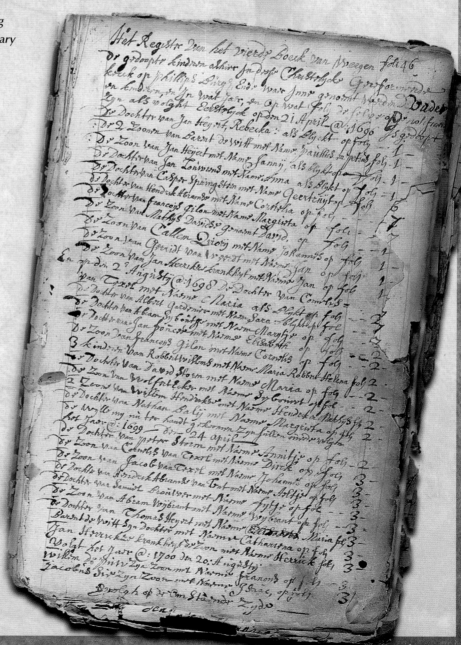

Scholar and Minister. Rev. David Cole, D.D., was a Greek scholar and longtime minister of the Reformed Church of Yonkers. Around 1900, he translated the *First Record Book* from Dutch into English.

Treasurer's Report. The first page shows 37 entries for baptisms, starting in 1697 and continuing into 1700.

FINALLY, A NEW DOMINE

" TWO WEATHERCOCKS
GRACED EACH END
OF THE CHURCH,
ONE PERCHED OVER
THE BELFRY, THE
OTHER OVER THE
CHANCEL. AS USUAL
WITH ECCLESIASTICAL
WEATHER COCKS, EACH
POINTED A DIFFERENT
WAY; AND THERE
WAS A PERPETUAL
CONTRADICTION
BETWEEN THEM ON
ALL POINTS OF WINDY
DOCTRINE; EMBLEMATIC,
ALAS! OF THE CHRISTIAN
PROPENSITY TO SCHISM
AND CONTROVERSY."

—WASHINGTON IRVING,
"WOLFERT'S ROOST," 1855

In the twenty years the manor church was without a regular pastor following Domine Bertholf's retirement, baptisms somehow continued as usual, two to four times a year. The consistory made payment to ministers, but their names were not recorded. Then in 1744 **Domine Johannes Ritzema,** thirty-six, from East Friesland was called to become the minister of the Dutch Church of New York City. In that same year he took over the supervision of churches that had no *domine* of their own, including the Philipsburg church.

A large new generation had grown into middle age since Domine Bertholf left, and the population had boomed. One writer compared a tax list with church records, and estimated that about 144 heads of household were living in Philipsburg by 1732. About 45 percent were of Dutch origin, 25 percent English, 13 percent French Huguenots, 6 percent Germans, and 6 percent Belgian Walloons, plus a scattering of other Europeans. Enslaved Africans were probably few outside Upper Mills, which, by this time, was functioning as a town. The manor church was thriving. About forty children were baptized each year.

Also during this time came growing controversy in Dutch Reformed churches in the colony. Two debates roiled the denomination in the eighteenth century, centering on the creation of a Reformed Church in America to govern colonial churches, and a switch from Dutch to English language in the pulpit, an attempt to counter the decline in attendance by young people, especially in the city. The first was not resolved until just before the Revolution, when the independence advocates gained the upper hand and settled the matter. The second controversy was settled church by church, if not by agreement, then through the inevitability of time.

In 1755, discussions over American independence for the church focused on establishment of a Dutch university. When a proposal was made for a Dutch

Population Boom. The Philipsburg settlement saw slow growth in the early years. In 1697, 20 poor families with no more than 100 members lived on the manor. Soon after the turn of the century, this began to change. By 1705, there were 200-plus residents; by 1712, there were 348, including 39 enslaved Africans. Before the Revolution, Philipsburg Manor had 1,100 to 1,500 people. Illustration: From *A School History of the United States*, 1879.

college to train Dutch Reformed ministers in America, Domine Ritzema proposed instead a Dutch professorship of divinity be created at New York's new Anglican college, King's College (now Columbia). He was a King's College trustee, and perhaps hoped to fill the professorship himself. It was an unpopular proposal that didn't go anywhere. In 1771, Queen's College in New Brunswick, N.J., opened its doors and began preparing young men for the Dutch Reformed ministry. It later became Rutgers College and the New Brunswick Theological Seminary.

The church at Philipsburg stayed out of that debate, but about ten years later congregants made their opinions known on the subject of English-language preaching. Some feared it would lead to the loss of the doctrines, the mode of worship, the government, and even the very name of the church itself. Robert Bolton, author of the comprehensive *History of the County of Westchester,* later wrote, "Rev. Ritzema, at this time the officiating minister at Sleepy Hollow, uniformly acted throughout this trying period as the friend of the English." Ritzema's support of English-language church services may have still rankled twenty years later, when the next pastor after Ritzema would shock the congregation by conducting a baptism in English (see chapter 7).

In 1776, Domine Ritzema left the city, probably for Tarrytown, where he stayed for two years. On April 28, 1777, he signed his name to the last entry written in Dutch in the minutes of the *First Record Book*. The church's second *domine* died, age eighty-six, in Kinderhook in 1794.

Calm Before the Storm

In the next decades, the little bell at the church at Philipsburg continued to ring out on a regular basis, welcoming worshippers. New generations took their seats on the uncomfortable benches. Like their parents, their lives revolved around faith, family and church.

Happily, many settlers lived to see their children and grandchildren enjoy a widening prosperity. They built new plank (instead of log) houses and planted flower gardens. They stuffed their attic storerooms with dried fish, sausages, corn, beans, pumpkins, potatoes, maple sugar, honey and every other good thing from land and river. No one was very poor, and the wealthiest counted their riches in full barnyards, granaries and storerooms. When a family suffered a setback, deacons distributed alms from the *arme-kas*, or poor fund. Congregants were generous, and treasurers sometimes borrowed from the fund to pay the *domine*'s salary, always balancing accounts later.

Growing Prosperity. Full larders were a sign of wealth. Photo: Westchester County Historical Society.

Their landlord—in turn Frederick Philipse's son Adolph, grandson Frederick II, and great-grandson Frederick III—was fair and easygoing and would even make loans to help tenant farmers improve their farms. The farmers responded with their loyalty, abiding by their verbal lifetime leases and staying for generations. By 1775, the *First Record Book* listed 390 members, 425 marriages and more than 2,200 baptisms. Apparently, none of Frederick and Margaret Philipse's immediate descendants became members of the church, though several were interred in the family crypt there.

Also by 1775, the beginnings of a town had planted itself a mile south of the church, beside the river. The little hamlet of Tarrytown, a dozen or so houses, probably took its name from *tarwe dorp*, Dutch for "wheat town." It had a local government of trustees, a town supervisor, a superintendent of highways and the alms house, and a "fence-viewer," whose job it was to prevent arguments between neighbors by ensuring fences were kept in good repair.

Members of the church continued to be central to the community's well-being. For instance, from his boat landing, Daniel Martling ran market sloops to and from Manhattan. On market days, farmers stopped in at the Van Tassel Tavern and the Couenhoven Inn to enjoy a glass of cider and catch up on news. All that, however, was about to change.

CHAPTER 4

BEHIND THE
HEADSTONES

Rocks wrested from surrounding fields are the first gravestones. And soon many of the families of the Old Dutch Church—the Eckers, the Van Tassels and Van Winkles, the Martlings, Requas and Odells, among others—were immortalized differently: with artistic sandstone carvings, now considered folk art. These stones are among the rare artifacts of our country's early history. Weathered and worn, cracked and crumbling, they are truly a national treasure! Alas, no marker for the Headless Horseman, but his hoofprints run up the hill to the grave of storyteller Washington Irving. And, though mute, the stones at the Old Dutch still reveal enchanting tales about people of the past.

War Heroes. In all, 190 veterans rest at the Old Dutch Burying Ground, including more than 70 Revolutionary soldiers.

SACRED GROUND

A rough fieldstone pulled from rocky soil. A name chiseled perhaps by a grieving father, or by a local blacksmith or a sign painter. A date now worn with time.

The words: "Here is Elizabeth Guions' grave."

This grave marker at the Old Dutch Church for infant Elizabeth Guion, her life swept away in 1755 by some unexpected ailment or epidemic, takes on new significance today. Her two short years on earth are poignantly recorded on the oldest inscribed gravestone in one of the country's oldest graveyards. The anguish feels palpable, with the uneven, inexpertly chiseled letters; an "s" and apostrophe awkwardly end up on the third line with the word "grave."

Oldest Stone. Elizabeth Guion only lived two years.

Sweeping away layers of time, this simple memorial for Elizabeth Guion speaks to her family's loss. Her father, Amon, was a miller at the Philipse gristmill and a Huguenot, among the descendants of French Protestant settlers who fled mounting persecutions by Catholic monarchs in their native country. Amon's marriage to Sara Krankheyt (she was of Dutch heritage, born on the manor) was recorded at the Old Dutch Church, as was the joyful baptism for Elizabeth and her siblings. The family was all too soon in mourning.

Most early fieldstone and wood markers have long since disappeared from the three-acre Old Dutch Burying Ground, the very place that Washington Irving made famous in America's best-loved ghost story, "The Legend of Sleepy Hollow." The earliest pioneer burials are thought to be before 1650. (A Native American

"TOGETHER WE PACED THE AMPLE CHURCHYARD. WITH DEEP VENERATION WOULD HE [DIEDRICH KNICKERBOCKER] TURN DOWN THE WEEDS AND BRANCHES THAT OBSCURED THE MODEST BROWN GRAVESTONES, HALF SUNK IN EARTH, ON WHICH WERE RECORDED, IN DUTCH, THE NAMES OF THE PATRIARCHS OF ANCIENT DAYS, THE ACKERS, THE VAN TASSELS, AND THE VAN WARTS. AS WE SAT ON ONE OF THE TOMBSTONES, HE RECOUNTED TO ME THE EXPLOITS OF MANY OF THESE WORTHIES."

—WASHINGTON IRVING, "SLEEPY HOLLOW," *KNICKERBOCKER,* 1839

burial site also existed nearby.) Some 180 burials occurred before 1700.

A first-person account of these burials was reported by Catherine Van Cortlandt. Her father-in-law Pierre, the first lieutenant governor of New York State until 1795 and owner of adjoining Cortlandt Manor, told her that he had seen "several coffins under the church bearing old dates, and, as near as [she could] recall it, one which he saw of a child, covered with green cloth or baize, and the date in brass-headed nails [from the sixteen] fifties." The Philipse family crypt under the church floorboards was actually built in the 1680s, when the church foundation was laid. Lord Frederick Philipse, who constructed the church, was buried in the crypt in 1702 and eventually at least fifteen others, including his son Adolph and grandson Frederick II. The crypt is not open for public viewing.

No identifying details remain at another burying ground west of the church for Philipsburg slaves. "Unfortunately, the slave burying place was destroyed when the land on the west side of Route 9 opposite the Old Dutch Burying Ground was developed," writes Patrick Raftery in his book, *The Cemeteries of Westchester County*. Raftery quotes Rev. John Knox Allen, pastor of the Old Dutch from 1870 to 1920, who observed: "Occasionally, in digging in that soil, a skull is found, or some relic of the dead."

Folk Art! The oldest sandstone marker in the Burying Ground is an early work of New York City stonecarver John Zuricher. It belongs to Mary Drake, who died in 1757, at 32.

46

A LEGACY IN FOLK ART

With increased prosperity, the Philipsburg farmers could soon afford to pay for reddish-brown sandstone markers from quarries across the Hudson in northern New Jersey and Rockland County. The use of this easy-to-carve and durable stone started a new practice for burying the dead at the Old Dutch Burying Ground: artistic gravestones.

Surprisingly, these decorated stones—with cherubic faces known as soul effigies—are considered some of the earliest and most enduring examples of American folk art, which was produced by craftsmen–artists. In 1983, *Reflections of Faith: Religious Folk Art in America*, at the Museum of American Folk Art in New York City, was the first national exhibition to explore America's rich heritage of the folk artist's spiritual inspiration. Along with paintings and other decorative items, the exhibit displayed five gravestones similar to markers at the Old Dutch Church, with the oldest from 1767.

How do gravestones figure as art? Here's what the exhibit brochure says:

> *Firmly rooted in the crafts tradition, folk art often takes a utilitarian or decorative item—from anonymously produced shop signs and figures, gravestones, weather vanes and decoys, to delicate crewelwork, patchwork and hand-painted tinware.*

The Old Dutch Church's decorative gravestones are indeed a national treasure! The primitive art conveys beliefs and customs of the time, attitudes toward death, and favorite pious sayings.

Soulful Look. Among the early stones in Dutch is this one for Sara Fochee Enters (d. 1769), one of Zuricher's later stones.

Crown of Righteousness. An effigy atop Peter Brush's grave (d. 1801) mourns his loss, age 38. This gravestone is by Solomon Brewer.

47

Myth or Fact

Is Washington Irving Buried at the Old Dutch?

The final resting place of our famous storyteller is ... not at Old Dutch. This 1866 engraving depicts the Irving family plot just up the hill at the Sleepy Hollow Cemetery. Both graveyards share a common border. Irving was a member of Christ Church in Tarrytown, but in the 1840s he considered buying a burial plot at the Old Dutch Church. Then a woody hill above the Old Dutch Church in a new cemetery (incorporation 1849) caught his fancy and he bought a family plot for $174. Shortly after Irving's death on November 28, 1859, Rev. John A. Todd, pastor of Tarrytown's Second Reformed Dutch Church, recalled Irving's "most solemn and tender expression of his anticipation in regard to death. Only five days before he closed his eyes forever, he stood by his mother's grave and pointing to the spot by the side of it which he had selected for his own, he said calmly to the friend at his side: 'I shall soon be there.'"

Among the oldest gravestones, for instance, are eleven in Dutch, the language of the church's first hundred years. They include that of Catriena Ecker Van Tassel, who died in 1793. With an inscription in Dutch, a verse in English and a motto in Latin, her stone illustrates the enduring use of Dutch language and customs well into the mid- and late-1700s, more than a hundred years after 1664, when the English took over the colony from the Dutch.

As an insight into beliefs, the quaint soul effigies with wings springing from the sides of the face are meant to symbolize the soul's flight to heaven. Moreover, the graves are carefully laid out with a predominant east-west orientation. Heads are to the west with footstones, if existing, to the east and marked with the person's initials. Why? According to tradition, on the Day of Judgment the bodies of the righteous would rise up to face Christ in the east.

By the late 1700s, soul effigies went out of style, replaced by inscriptions with epitaphs (a scriptural quotation or poem). Because the Dutch Reformed Church didn't dwell on mortality and instead emphasized resurrection of the body, the images of skulls, bones and other dour symbols of death never became popular. Nor did carvings of Christ or Mary, since at that time in the eighteenth century much religious imagery was considered a "false idol." Eventually, however, images such as weeping willows (mourning) and classical urns (for ashes) came into style. The type of stone in vogue changed over time too. Replacing the red sandstone were white marble markers in the 1800s and granite in the late 1800s and 1900s.

Irving Connection. Susanna Ecker (d. 1767, gravestone above) married Wolfert Ecker III, whose family's name was immortalized by Washington Irving in "Wolfert's Roost." Irving bought what was once the Wolfert family cottage and tranformed it into Sunnyside.

All of the seventy-six soldiers, commemorated in the Revolutionary Soldiers Monument on nearby Battle Hill, were buried at the Old Dutch Burying Ground; their graves flutter with American flags. The honor roll includes Col. James Hammond, who commanded the local militia throughout the war, and numerous local Patriot heroes (see chapter 5 for details). Soon, with space for interments becoming scarce (1,073 and 1,940 burials in the eighteenth and nineteenth centuries, respectively), a larger cemetery was needed.

Washington Irving and his cronies helped to establish what's now called Sleepy Hollow Cemetery on adjoining land. It opened in 1849 and now covers a hundred peaceful acres overlooking the Hudson. And by 1860, most local burials took place in the larger cemetery.

Today, though space remains limited, church members can choose the Old Dutch Church's historic burying ground as their final resting place. Up the hillside in the Sleepy Hollow Cemetery are well-known neighbors: steel magnate Andrew Carnegie, cosmetic entrepreneur Elizabeth Arden, labor leader Samuel Gompers and oil tycoon William Rockefeller, among others. And, of course, America's beloved storyteller and statesman Washington Irving. In the churchyard that he made famous, his Headless Horseman is said to gallop about by night, past little Elizabeth Guion and the early Dutch settlers, past the Revolutionary heroes, past the prized folk-art stones, past the newer graves ...

Such a sense of wonder awaits the visitor to this still drowsy, enchanting place. Time truly embraces those slumbering in this sacred burial place that Washington Irving made world famous, a land called Sleepy Hollow....

1,600 Requas and Counting

When the Requa family held a reunion in Tarrytown in 1978, with some 180 out of 1,600 descendants attending, the local newspaper called their story an "American classic with moments of high drama, courage, patriotism and tragedy." The following is an adaptation of Marcia Moore's article in the Tarrytown Daily News.

"The Requas' story begins near Rochelle, France. According to family legend, which may have been embellished with the passing of more than 330 years, 12 families of French Huguenots, or Protestants, lived in hiding to avoid persecution from the Roman church. They concealed forbidden Bibles in the bottoms of chairs and met in secret, but were discovered.

"A friend told the families of plans to massacre them. They stole away in the night, with their wagon wheels wrapped in cloth to muffle the sound. They were pursued and only ten families escaped. Among them was Claude Equier, his wife and their only child Gabriel. They may have fled to England first, or they may have boarded a ship directly for the American colonies, but Claude and his wife died of a fever before reaching the new land. Gabriel, an orphan at about age 12, grew up near New Rochelle, a Huguenot settlement, and married Jeanne, whose parents had also died on the passage to the colonies. About 1700, Jeanne gave birth to their only child, a son whom they named Claude in memory of Gabriel's father.

"Claude also grew up and married, and had eight children. Sometime between 1723 and 1729, he moved his family west to lease 296 acres of prime Hudson Valley farmland in the Tarrytown area from the Philipse family. Although Claude Equier was reportedly 'so Frenchy in his talk' that the Dutch settlers of Tarrytown couldn't understand him, he performed an act which insured the singularity of his name for later generations: He changed it to Glode Requa, a version that tripped more easily off the tongues of his Dutch neighbors. When his oldest son was born, he named him Glode Requa.

"Over the years Requas—all descended from this couple—became small business owners, bankers, ministers and boat captains—and, surprisingly, the name Glode Requa still exists!"

Long Legacy! Joining the Requas is Mrs. Henry Requa, married in 1883. (Photo: The Historical Society Serving Sleepy Hollow and Tarrytown.) Above, right: The 1806 gravestone of Glode Requa, who was given the new spelling of the family name at his birth.

Three Carvers. A square-faced soul effigy, as seen on the 1761 Dutch gravestone for Abraham Martling (top), is characteristic of John Zuricher's work. Solomon Brewer carved a solemn effigy on the stone for John Yurks (1789, middle). Brewer's son James chiseled the inscription, now hard to read, for his master-carver father (1824, bottom); at the time soul effigies had already gone out of style!

THE MASTER CARVERS

The primitive carvings of two stone sculptors—Solomon Brewer and John Zuricher—still stand out as exemplary folk art at the Old Dutch Burying Ground, more than 200 years later!

Solomon Brewer was one of the most prolific carvers of headstones at the church and in all of Westchester County. Born in 1746 in Springfield, Mass., he was initially a farmer or cabinetmaker, or both, and began gravestone carving probably in the late 1760s. According to *The Old Dutch Burying Ground of Sleepy Hollow* (1926), he was "said to be a member of the Boston Tea Party" and served during the Revolutionary War in the militia. Not long after the war Brewer moved from New England with his wife and large family and settled in the Hudson Valley, living in Tarrytown and eventually purchasing a farm in Greenburgh, N.Y. To supplement his income—he averaged just about ten to twelve headstones yearly, not enough work to support his family—he was a stonemason, schoolteacher, auctioneer and census-taker. He was even Greenburgh's town clerk.

At the Old Dutch Church, more than 200 of Brewer's stones still grace the graveyard. What's so distinctive about his style? Following a common practice in the 1700s, most stones are decorated with winged soul effigies, which symbolized the soul's transcendence in heaven. Other qualities characterize his carvings: his soul effigies have a round face, a long bulbous nose and downturned eyes at the outer corners, giving a mournful look. Whorled wings spring from either side of the face. Often a crown of righteousness sits on the soul's head with, according to Scripture, its promise of redeeming souls in heavenly bliss. Another trademark: In his chiseled lettering Brewer joined the letters "AD," found next to the year of the person's death.

"For the most part, Brewer remained loyal to his formula: simple, engraved decoration on stones of modest size," wrote historian Gray Williams in an article for *Markers XI, Journal of the Association for Gravestone Studies*. "He apparently offered a comprehensive service to his customers, including a repertoire of traditional verses.

Williams continued, "Some are very well known such as: 'Death is a debt, to nature due, which I have paid and so must you.' And probably the most famous of all: 'Reader behold as you pass by, as you are now so once was I. As I am now so you must be. Prepare for death and follow me.'"

Thanks Be to Preservation!

Nearly all the graves of the first hundred years of burials have disappeared as markers eroded. With each, a little history is lost to us.

To preserve the rich history of the remaining stones, the church has twice undertaken massive efforts to map and inventory the graveyard. As a result, two books document the findings: *The Old Dutch Burying Ground of Sleepy Hollow* (1926) and *The Old Dutch Burying Ground of Sleepy Hollow: A Record of the Early Gravestones and Their Inscriptions* (1953). As part of the latter effort, William G. Perry, a Boston architect, selected 106 of the neediest stones to restore and worked closely with the Obelisk Waterproofing Company in the 1940s and 1950s to make necessary repairs.

Of special concern to Perry were the stresses from frost, grassfires, poor drainage and internal pressure to the old brownish-red sandstone, which "may conceal its defects until nearly the last disastrous moment when the face falls away." In short, stone "shells" and flakes as water gets into cracks and freezes.

In contrast, marble markers are more durable but are susceptible to surface erosion, especially from acid rain. "Its principal enemy is carbon dioxide gas present in the air, which when it strikes a damp surface of marble becomes carbonic acid," wrote Perry.

Helping Hands. In 1990, Walter J. Harrison (left) and William Lent, president and vice president of Friends of Old Dutch, removed the headstone of Col. James Hammond to clean and reset it; this was one of many restoration projects by the Friends. Photo: Westchester County Historical Society.

In 1985, the Friends of the Old Dutch Burying Ground came into existence to promote interest in the graveyard and help ensure its preservation. Formed under the auspices of the Junior League of Westchester-on-Hudson, the Friends more recently published *Tales of the Old Dutch Burying Ground,* a booklet of legends and lore associated with Old Dutch. The organization expanded its mission in 2010 to include the historic church as well.

Maintenance, of course, is an ongoing job. Additional preservation efforts will always be needed to maintain the legendary stone graveyard treasures for all to enjoy in the centuries ahead!

Sayings Set in Stone

My cares are past
My bones at rest
GOD took my life
When he thought best.
—Ann Couenhoven, 1797

Corruption, earth and worms
Shall but refine my flesh
Till my triumphant spirit comes
To put it on afresh.
—Captain John Hilleker, 1824

Tho boisterous winds and Neptune's
Wave have tossed me too and fro
By God's decree you plainly see
I am harbored here below.
—James Barnerd, 1768

When living
He was respected
And in death he is lamented
By all who knew him
Go Reader
And imitate his example.
—Gideon McChain, 1829

The righteous shall enter into peace:
They shall rest in their beds, each one
walking in his uprightness
—Jane Van Winkel, 1799
    from sandstone no longer extant

By the late 1790s, people had lost interest in soul effigies. For a while, stones with lettering only—no effigy—were in vogue, so Brewer started to use elaborate Gothic script and other simple touches. "For children's stones," explained Williams, "he developed an odd little decoration composed of a double-ended banner, surmounted by a heart." By 1817, his sons **James and Horace Brewer** learned how to carve and joined the family business. James, for instance, created a simple double sandstone marker, no effigies—its epitaph ringing with "In vain your tears ye faithful mourners rise; your friends are safely lodg'd within the skies"—for Cornelius and Elizabeth Van Tassel, who both died in the 1820s.

Appropriately, Brewer himself is buried along with his family at the Old Dutch Burying Ground. His marble stone, carved by James, did not have soul effigies, but recorded faithfully that he "departed this life March the 18th, AD 1824, Aged 77 Years, 9 Months and 14 days." On the gravestone is this verse, one that the master carver himself used on the stone for farmer Glode Requa: "Life is at best a narrow bound, that heaven allows to men; while pain and sorrow fills the round, of threescore years and ten."

Another well-known artistic carver deserves mention: **John Zuricher**. He and his wife, Elizabeth, along with their ten children, lived in New York City. Considered one of the first New York stonecutters, he kept his stoneyard not far from the Hudson, and primarily carved between 1749 and 1778. As a stonemason, he cut milestones for the post roads in New York and Westchester, and reportedly cut cornices for City Hall in Manhattan. During the Revolution when the British occupied New York, Zuricher fled up the Hudson to Rockland County.

As for Zuricher's gravestones at the Old Dutch Church, they sport picturesque soul effigies—sometimes square, oval or pear-shaped—that bear distinctive puffy cheeks and can be spotted on several stones. He carved the marker for Abraham Martling (1761), whose farm was divided and became the heart of the village of Tarrytown; carver Solomon Brewer, however, made the gravestone for Martling's son Abraham (1786). Nobody knows where Zuricher himself is buried or who carved his stone, only that he died in May 1784.

Fortunately, John Zuricher's artistry lives on—in the endearing soul effigies bearing thick eyebrows and pudgy cheeks on the stones he crafted for others.

Death Conquers All. So states the Latin inscription on the gravestone for Catriena Ecker Van Tassel (d. 1793), carved by Solomon Brewer. Her name, though similar in spelling to that of Katrina Van Tassel in Irving's "Legend," appears to be as far as the connection goes.

AN EARLY DUTCH FUNERAL

In 1697, when the Old Dutch Church formally organized, its members chose Jan Ecker as the first deacon and later as an elder in 1702–04, and assigned various duties. (His brother Wolfert, who owned a small house that Washington Irving eventually bought and renamed Sunnyside, was the subject of "Wolfert's Roost.") The church appointed Ecker to help conduct church services and funerals if no minister was available. Early records indicated that he would hold funerals "in a Christian manner, and that he walked before the procession to the grave."

An account by a traveler to Albany in 1789, recorded in Alice Morse Earle's book *Colonial Days in Old New York* (1896), sheds light on funeral customs:

> *None attend [a funeral] without a previous invitation. At the appointed hour they meet at the neighboring houses or stoops until the corpse is brought out. Ten or twelve persons are appointed to take the bier altogether and are not to be relieved. The clerk then desires the gentlemen (for ladies never walk to the grave, nor even attend the funeral unless a near relation)*

A Familiar Figure. The late William Lent, sexton, church historian and popular guide.

to fall into the procession. They go to the grave and return to the house of mourning in the same order. Here the tables are handsomely set with cold and spiced wine, tobacco and pipes, and candles, paper, etc., to light them. The house of mourning is soon converted into a house of feasting.

With an emphasis on feasting and celebrating the person, a Dutch funeral was a festive event, one that was saved for long in advance. The poor were not excluded. Dutch churches, including the Philipsburg Manor church, had a poor fund. An example of how the church might help: In 1695, a Dutch church in Albany, N.Y., gave a local family 40 guilders a month to provide a poor Dutchman named Claes Janse with *logement, kost, drank, wassen* (lodging, food, drink, washing). When he died, the church paid for his funeral; this practice was followed for any indigent Dutchman. "With a good dry coffin, a good dry grave, and a far from dry funeral," wrote Earle in *Colonial Days in Old New York,* "Claes's days, though he were of the church poor, ended in honor." His itemized bill was dutifully recorded:

Dead shirt and cap, 16 guilders	5 gallons Madeira wine, 42 guilders
Winding sheet,14 guilders	Tobacco, pipes, and sugar, 4 guilders, 10 stuyvers
Making coffin, 24 guilders	3 cartloads sand for grave, 1 guilder, 10 stuyvers
2 half vats good beer, 30 guilders	1 lb. nails, cartage coffin, 3 guilders, 10 stuyvers
6 bottles rum, 22 guilders	Grave digging, 3 guilders

In addition to the Albany church paying approximately 160 guilders for the funeral, its deacons supplied three dry boards for the coffin and use of a pall.

For tenants on Philipsburg Manor, funerals were held in the person's front parlor, also known as a *doed-kamer,* or dead room. The cost for refreshments could be significant. Pallbearers carrying the coffin to the graveyard were often given gifts: gloves, a mourning ring, a linen scarf, a handkerchief, or a decorative "monkey" spoon, which the Dutch also used to commemorate a birth or marriage and that hung from a hook like a monkey swinging from its tail.

Rev. John M. Ferris arrived at Old Dutch in 1849. He spoke about a curious custom he encountered at his first funeral, which was for a poor workingman:

As I drove up to his cottage, I saw the carriages of some gentlemen of the vicinity. The sight was startling. Was I to speak before Mr. Irving, Mr. Hamilton, Mr. Paulding? But as I entered the house my fears were allayed. The men I feared were not there. That was kind to the gathering of workingmen and women. It left them to hold their service without restraint. The carriages were there to convey the working people to the graveyard. It was customary to send carriages to the homes of workingmen they knew.

What Is It? This 150-year-old bier transported caskets through a rear window into the church!

Epidemic of Epidemics!

An outbreak of yellow fever in Manhattan in 1798 was what prompted Washington Irving's parents to send their son, then fifteen, to Tarrytown and thus set the stage for his poking around the bucolic countryside and later writing "The Legend of Sleepy Hollow," among other stories. As the Old Dutch Burying Ground attests in its headstones, the 1700s and 1800s were thick with cholera, fevers and flu, and other horrible epidemics. During this period, for instance, North America was gripped by the smallpox epidemic of 1775–1782, which killed an estimated 130,000 people.

Several years before Irving's visit to the area, the powerful blow of an epidemic within one family was captured in a heart-wrenching, though picturesque, marker. In 1794, Jacob and Catalyna Couenhoven lost three children in nine days. Their triple-arched stone is topped by three soul effigies carved by Solomon Brewer, and the epitaph says "How lovely & pleasant were they in their lives; & in their deaths they were not divided."

Jemima, the first wife of John Dutcher, saw seven of her children die before she passed away herself in 1807 at the youthful age of thirty-one. Her children, likely stricken by various epidemics, ranged from five days (Edward, 1795) to two years of age (Charlotte, 1802). The verse on her gravestone records her agony:

> Ye friends who lately saw my bloom,
> Here now behold me in my tomb!
> My children dear once round my bed,
> In number seven with me are dead;
> The dropping tear is not amiss,
> Well may ye weep o'er such a scene as this.

The uncertainty of life also struck Rev. Thomas Smith, who for twenty-nine years was pastor of the Old Dutch Church. His daughters Mary, nineteen, and Jemima, sixteen, passed away within two days of each other in September 1813. The final lines on their double tombstone: "Perfect in life, they from their heavenly home, look down and smiling beckon you to come."

Triple Stone. An epidemic wiped out three Couenhoven children in 1794 within days of each other: Cornelius (five years), Jacob (three), and Winey (one).

55

Tales from the Graveyard

The most famous story set at Old Dutch is, of course, "The Legend of Sleepy Hollow." In America's favorite ghost story, Washington Irving says "one would think that there at least the dead could rest in peace." But other stories keep springing up from the graves …

A Pale, Blue-Eyed Man

The Old Dutch shelters the remains of many soldiers, but few generals. Sleepy Hollow village historian Henry Steiner tells the story of a villager who was once a New York theater critic and followed an unusual path to become a general:

Civil War. Badeau (right, standing) with then Gen. Ulysses S. Grant, who soon became the 18th U.S. president.

"General Adam Badeau was born in New York City in 1831. His parents later moved to Beekmantown, now Sleepy Hollow, and owned one of the three most imposing homes in that sprouting suburb.

"At the outset of the Civil War, Adam Badeau was a clerk at the State Department. He volunteered as an officer and by April 1862, held the rank of captain. A member of General Grant's staff suggested that Badeau would make a fine military secretary. Grant remembered him as 'a little pale, blue-eyed man, who wore spectacles and looking like a bent fo'-pence.' Badeau was duly ordered to report to Grant's headquarters near Vicksburg, but on that day was wounded. Sent to New York City to convalesce, Badeau was cared for by two theatrical friends: the famous actor, Edwin Booth, and his soon-to-be-infamous brother John Wilkes Booth!

"In February 1864, Badeau had sufficiently recovered to join Grant's staff, with the rank of lieutenant colonel. Badeau proved to be an intelligent and thorough military secretary. He served in the Wilderness and Appomattox campaigns and accompanied Grant at Lee's surrender. In a letter of May 1865, he writes of Grant, 'What a wonderful man he is. His goodness is greater than his greatness.'

"After the war, Badeau was a constant member of Grant's entourage. In 1869, he retired from the military with the rank of brigadier general as Grant moved into the White House. Badeau was appointed consul general to London from 1870 to 1881. And in 1877 and 1878 he toured the world with the former president. But by 1884 Badeau was out of a job, and Grant was financially wrecked, tainted with allegations of swindling and dying of throat cancer. Badeau agreed to help Grant with research on his memoirs. But by May 1885, they had fallen out over the book. Badeau complained bitterly over the 'drudgery' of the work and made an inappropriate proposal for compensation. Grant replied, 'You are petulant, your anger is easily aroused and you are overbearing even to me.' Grant soon died, and Badeau continued to write his own books—often about Grant." On March 19, 1895, Badeau died at age sixty-three and was interred at the Old Dutch Burying Ground.

Arise, Ye Dead!

Rev. John Knox Allen delighted in telling this tall tale: "There is a story, probably told concerning other places as well as this, concerning a man of unbalanced mind who was accustomed to go up to the old churchyard, look off at the graves and cry, 'Arise, ye dead, and come to judgment!'

A certain man put up a job on him. Once when the demented man made a visit, the other wrapped himself in a sheet and hid behind one of the tall headstones. When the crazy man cried, 'Arise, ye dead, and come to judgment!' he slowly and silently rose.

"The crazy man regarded him a minute and then said, 'You stand there until I call up the rest.'"

56

What Lies Beneath?

In June 1896, the pastor of the First Reformed Church, four members of the consistory and three members of the church decided to open the Old Dutch Church crypt. This was in preparation for celebrating the 200th anniversary of the Old Dutch's official organization. To reach it, they cut through the floorboards near the chancel rail. They found the coffins of the Philipse family, numbering no fewer than sixteen. Here, excerpted from *The Old Dutch Church of Sleepy Hollow,* is how Rev. Allen described the macabre adventure:

Watch Your Step! The Philipse family lies in a crypt under the church floorboards.

"In 1897 the Church was two hundred years old, and we observed the bicentennial. A tradition was that there were silver plates on the coffins of the Philipse family, who were buried in the vault up to the time of the American Revolution. Some of us felt there might be dates on these plates that would help us to fix the time of events. We determined to investigate, taking pains to keep the matter out of the New York papers, which would have denounced us as ghouls desecrating the resting place of the dead.

"One day we went up to the old building, taking with us a carpenter and a mason; we removed some seats and a part of the floor, found the brick vault, forced a way into it, put down a ladder, and with a lantern went below to explore. We found that coffins had been placed one above the other on the south and west sides of the vault, and the atmosphere was perfectly dry and sweet and clean.

"It was literally 'dust to dust,' only one skull remaining to show that human forms had been buried there. There were no silver plates; initials and dates had been made by driving bright-headed nails into coffin lids; fragments of the lids remained, but as you touched them they crumbled. We got no data whatever, though one of our number searched below for two hours.

"Another explorer was a very bald man, almost as bald as the skull we found. As he came up the ladder one time, his head just peering above the top of the vault, he announced in sepulchral tones, 'I am Lazarus.' This Lazarus thereupon proceeded to the gallery, where there is an old organ whose keys are something like the gap-toothed mouth of an old man, and there he endeavored to extract some music while his companions pursued their gruesome occupation."

Love Eternal

"I have wonderful plans for our life together," Jacob Romer told Frena Haerlager in the mid-1700s. But Jacob was just a poor tailor in their small Swiss village, and Frena's father objected. Only one solution made sense: run away to America. They were able to secure "free" passage on a ship to the new country by pledging to work several years without pay for a master in America.

Calamity struck. Frena and Jacob were indentured to two different masters and they lost contact. After earning his freedom, Jacob moved to Philipsburg Manor. All he knew about Frena was that she was indentured somewhere west of the Hudson.

A post rider who covered both sides of the river heard Jacob's story. "I'll see what I can discover on my next run up to Albany," he said. A short time later who trotted up on horseback behind the post rider? Frena. The monument erected by the Romers' descendants is prominent in the Burying Ground.

In the Dead of Night. On moonlit evenings the Headless Horseman has been spotted on this bridge over the Pocantico River. Photo: Matt Hill.

Myth or Fact

Does the Headless Horseman Roam Sleepy Hollow?

Each fall the churchyard is crowded with visitors in search of the Headless Horseman. Hoofprints are spotted. "The Legend of Sleepy Hollow" is performed at the darkened church. Suddenly a ghostly figure, a lady in white, appears outside the windows. Could the ghost of the Hessian soldier, his head shot off by a cannonball during some unnamed battle in the Revolutionary War, also be nearby, searching for his head? As storyteller Washington Irving says in "The Legend": "The dominant spirit that haunts this enchanted region is the apparition of a figure on horseback, without a head."

Alas, Irving never mentioned the location of the Headless Horseman's grave, only that he was buried in the churchyard. So, for the brave and gutsy, the best way to find the horseman may be to go to the Old Dutch Burying Ground between midnight and dawn on a night in the fall under a full harvest moon. Follow the hoofprints encircling the Old Dutch Church. You never know … you just might spot his ghost rising from some unmarked burial place.

Graveyard Witch or Patriot?

In colonial times, just about every village in the East had its witch, and Sleepy Hollow was no exception. According to legend, Hulda, the "witch" of Sleepy Hollow, received … a Christian burial.

Hulda was an immigrant from Bohemia. She gathered herbs, traded with the Indians, and kept a cow or two at her cabin, not far from the church. Sometimes a sick neighbor would find a basket of healing herbal potions at his door and suspect that Hulda was the donor. But because she was a stranger and lived alone, the cliquish Dutch viewed her with suspicion.

During the Revolution, this whole area was in the so-called Neutral Ground. This was a dangerous no-man's-land where farms were at risk of being plundered and burned by marauders from either side. No one was safe. So when Hulda's cows were stolen by Loyalist "cowboys," she took up her gun to join her neighbors—men and women alike—on road patrols. Alas, nobody wanted her around. One day she responded to a general alarm to help turn back a British landing party. Troops had come ashore from a transport and were headed north to Peekskill. Legend says that on Battle Hill, just at the top of the rise above the Burying Ground, she shot and killed several British soldiers before she was killed by a British bullet.

Witch or no witch, the community gave her a Christian burial. The decision to do so may have been influenced by searchers who, as legend has it, found a Bible in her cottage with her will inside. She left her small purse of gold to women whose husbands died fighting for the colonies' freedom. Her burial place is unmarked, by tradition, and located in the grassy area behind the church.

CHAPTER 5

REVOLUTIONARY WAR: SEVEN YEARS OF HELL, 1776–1783

During the Revolution, the Old Dutch was in the Neutral Ground, a buffer zone between the British in New York and the Patriots in the Hudson River Valley to the north. Yet warfare was waged around the church, which suspended services. The Albany Post Road, a conduit between the two armies, rumbled under wheels and marching feet, and on the hill above the churchyard, cannons guarded nearby Pocantico bridge. In late September 1780, the future of America hung on the actions of three young local farmers, likely church members, who crossed paths nearby with a British spy. And soon Gen. George Washington himself rested his troops in the churchyard.

Ye Olde Dutch Church, Sleepy Hollow, Tarrytown, N. Y. (In Colonial Time)

Sundays Before the Revolution. This postcard features Wordsworth Thompson's (1840–1896) artwork of the Philipsburg church, circa 1750. The door, however, wasn't moved to this location until 1837! Image: Westchester County Historical Society.

War Comes to Sleepy Hollow

Many Westchester farmers didn't rush to take part in the committees that grew up in opposition to the British. "The controversy between England and America, which began in 1763, did not affect the welfare of these farmers, and consequently their interest in the questions, so hotly debated in the city, was languid and confined to a very few," wrote Otto Hufeland in *Westchester County During the American Revolution 1775–1783*. Most Philipsburg Manor tenants had not taken a stand as of April 1775. Edward Countryman, author of *A People in Revolution,* said that of the 283 male tenants, 58 percent were uncommitted, 27 percent were royalists and 15 percent were revolutionaries.

But not all were apathetic or uninvolved. Some of the church families, such as the Deans and Martlings, joined the invasion force in Canada, well before the Declaration of Independence was signed. In general, wrote Henry Steiner, Sleepy Hollow village historian, "the more affluent were more likely to be or to become Loyalists in the struggle and the less affluent tended to be or become Whigs or Patriots."

In 1775 the Continental Congress asked New York to build up a militia to enforce order and keep the Loyalists under control. Lt. Col. James Hammond, forty-eight, a church member and tenant farmer on the manor, was commissioned and soon put in command of the 1st Westchester Regiment, made up of five companies formed from Philipsburg.

Congress provided no budget for the militias. Militiamen had to get their own weapons and ammunition. One of Hammond's early challenges was laxness. When two British men-of-war bristling with guns anchored in the Hudson off Tarrytown on July 12, 1776, a militia company of forty men was raised, as Hammond wrote to the State Convention, "on the supposition that the honorable Congress will immediately put the men under pay."

" NO PART OF THE COUNTRY WAS SO HARRIED, BY FRIEND AND FOE ALIKE."

— WASHINGTON IRVING

Col. James Hammond

Militia Commander
Died *1810*, Age 83

Brave Leader. The marble of Hammond's gravestone is pitted, hard to decipher. It is by carver Solomon Brewer. The neoclassical urn is unusual for Brewer but the epitaph is a popular one:

Epitaph

Tis finished tis done,
The spirit is fled.
The prisoner is gone,
The Warrior is dead.
The Christian is living
Through Jesus's love,
And gladly receiving,
A Kingdom above.

Roll Call. Militiamen from Philipsburg. Illustration: *Souvenir of the Revolutionary Soldiers' Monument Dedication.*

Reinforcements arrived from nearby Bedford. But the men's enthusiasm flagged after three days of watching and waiting. Hammond wrote General Washington asking for reinforcements, because the men "are continually going away without leave, to take care of their harvests."

But when the fighting started in Westchester County, most of the church congregation committed to the Patriot cause. In time the farmers' "obstinate patriotism" would exasperate the British authorities, leading British general Sir William Howe to exclaim, "I can do nothing with this Dutch population. I can neither buy them with money nor conquer them with force."

James Hammond remained in command of the 1st Westchester Regiment throughout the war, except for the year he spent in a British prison. His arrest came after General Washington stopped at his home one night to consult with him. A Loyalist neighbor who spotted Washington entering the Hammond home rushed off to inform the British. The next morning a heavy pounding on the door roused the Hammonds from sleep. When the colonel opened the door, two cannons and several angry British soldiers confronted him.

"Where is General Washington?" demanded an officer. Fortunately, after the meeting the previous night, Washington had continued on his journey to American headquarters in White Plains. In their fury, the British took Colonel Hammond and locked him up in Brooklyn. He escaped after a year and returned to the regiment.

MANY HEROES

In his *Chronicles of Tarrytown and Sleepy Hollow* (1897), writer Edgar Mayhew Bacon provides us with this insight into how the families living around Tarrytown and Sleepy Hollow protected themselves. The Van Tassels and the others cited by Bacon were the backbone of the Old Dutch Church:

> When the war for Independence was declared, the majority of the men were farmers, who knew how to handle a gun, who could stalk a deer, or encounter a bear with skill and courage.
>
> Such people, abandoned by the necessities of war to the tender mercies of marauders and stock thieves, were not long in devising ways to defend themselves. A sort of home guard, in which it is said that women as well as men did duty, was organized to picket the highway, and check the raids of cowboys and skinners. [Cowboys were Loyalist cattle rustlers, and skinners were Patriot marauders who "skinned" farms of provisions.] Some patrolled the river in whale-boats, and were a serious annoyance to the British.

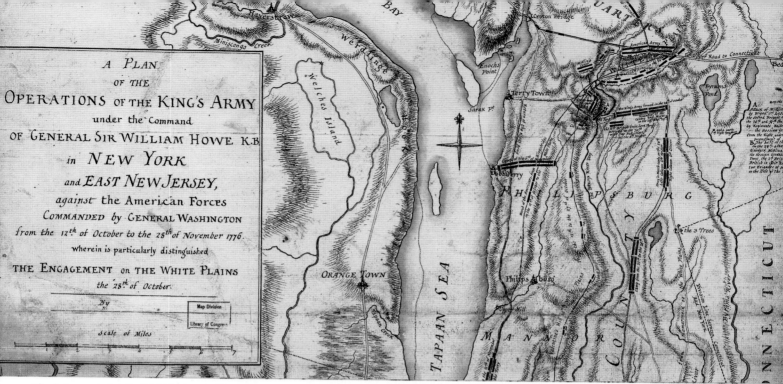

King's Army. A detail of British Gen. William Howe's plan of operations in 1776 shows troop movements east of Tarrytown in the Battle of White Plains.
Map reproduction: Norman B. Leventhal Map Center at the Boston Public Library.

Many locals joined the militia, or the Continental army, and suffered and died. Van Tassels, Van Warts, Sees, Requas, Martlings, Couenhovens, Deans, and others became locally celebrated for personal courage. "We must wonder that so small a settlement could produce so large a number of heroes," Bacon wrote.

How the Old Dutch Fared

Churches did not get much respect in the Revolution. When the Continental army pulled out of Manhattan, Gen. George Washington ordered bells to be stripped from churches, as much to deprive the British of this resource for making ammunition as to supply the Continental army of same. This led the congregation of St. Paul's Church in Eastchester (now Mount Vernon) to bury its bell for safekeeping. The British turned dissenting churches into prisons, hospitals and, in one case, a riding school.

In the Hudson River Valley, partisanship in the pulpit invited reprisals. British troops burned the church in Kingston, built in 1680, only eighty miles away and the site of fiery preaching in support of independence. Under Gov. William Tryon's "desolation warfare" policy in the Neutral Ground in late 1777, he turned Loyalist marauders loose to ransack the property of rebel civilian leaders and terrorize families, and troops burned parts of Tarrytown. The Old Dutch Church's location on the Albany Post Road left it highly exposed.

> " DEPLETED GRANARIES AND EMPTY SMOKE-HOUSES BROUGHT THE PEOPLE OFTEN TO THE VERGE OF STARVATION, AND THEY DETERIORATED FROM A PROSPEROUS LITTLE COMMUNITY TO A WRETCHED HANDFUL OF HUNGRY OUTCASTS, HOLDING THEIR INCH OF GROUND BY FORCE OF CUNNING AND SKILL."
>
> —EDGAR MAYHEW BACON, *CHRONICLES OF TARRYTOWN AND SLEEPY HOLLOW*, 1897

Myth or Fact

Bullet Holes?

The appearance of bullet-sized holes in the copper ball on the belfry weather vane brings to mind this story from a 1922 New York Times *article: Some years ago, a repairman at work on the roof spent an afternoon loosening the ball and repositioning it so it would agree with the tradition, which said that the British sharpshooter whose bullets pierced it had fired from the Albany Post Road. But the roofer was unaware that the road had changed course since the Revolution!*

Battle Scars? Two small holes in the copper ball are visible in this 1991 photo, taken during roof repairs. Photo: Westchester County Historical Society.

Even though its doors were locked and its bell silenced, the church was a witness to history. Troops marched by, marauders galloped by, and solitary travelers hurried by, fearful to be seen on the unsafe road. Skirmishes took place on the Post Road bordering the church's once-peaceful grounds. On the hill above the Burying Ground, Patriots planted a battery of cannons to defend the approaches to the Pocantico bridge below. Lawless acts of terror and violence—and the occasional shining act of bravery—were visited on soldiers and civilians alike.

Why the church wasn't trashed and burned is a mystery. Perhaps the British left it alone because Frederick Philipse III, the third lord of the manor, was a Loyalist. Its location in Neutral Ground made it unusable as a prison, storehouse or barracks, the fate of Dutch churches in the city. Unlike the Kingston church, no partisan minister rallied the Patriots from the Philipsburg pulpit. Domine Ritzema, the Old Dutch's part-time pastor for more than forty years, left New York City at the outbreak of the Revolution to eventually settle in Kinderhook. Some of the congregation also left the manor. But most did not abandon their farms, at least not in the beginning.

Without their church, the Philipsburg families still had Bible study and prayer. God had brought their forebears through many dangers, and this generation would pray hard to God that he would do the same for them.

FREDERICK PHILIPSE III, TRAITOR

Perhaps it did not surprise the congregation of the Old Dutch Church when the third lord of the manor sided with the Tories.

Frederick Philipse III had long since removed himself from Upper Mills by leasing it out. He continued to collect rents from his tenants and lived the sedentary life of a gentleman in Philipse Manor Hall at Lower Mills, in Yonkers. He and his wife, Elizabeth Williams Rutgers, daughter of an Englishman, liked to entertain in their lavishly decorated house. Colonel Philipse, as he was called (he received the commission while a young man in militia training and it stuck), was so overweight that his wife seldom traveled in the same carriage with him.

Fled to England. This painting by John Wollaston, circa 1750, is said to be of Frederick Philipse III, the only manor lord in Westchester County to remain loyal to the king. Illustration: New-York Historical Society.

Philipse served in the Assembly—a family tradition—but he wasn't driven by politics. He was an ardent Episcopalian. He and his family built the stone St. John's Church in Yonkers in 1752, also donating 250 acres of land and constructing a rectory.

John Jay, the first chief justice of the United States and a contemporary of Philipse, said of him, "He was a well-tempered, amiable man, and a kind, benevolent landlord. He had a [taste] for gardening, planting, etc., and employed much time and money in that way." Jay thought Philipse had been inclined to favor the Patriots but was persuaded to favor the Loyalists.

In any case, in April 1775, Philipse was an active opponent of the Continental Congress, his signature heading a list of more than 300 men on a petition to protest "unlawful congresses and committees." It read in part, "We are determined at the hazard of our lives and properties to support the king and constitution." Some of his tenants signed though later changed their minds. The petition and others like it were derided by Patriots as a "Declaration of Dependence."

The next year Colonel Philipse was called up before the New York Committee on Conspiracies to answer questions about his allegiance. He declined on account of ill health and was arrested on George Washington's orders. While paroled, he fled to New York City to live behind British lines, and in 1779 the New York legislature declared him a traitor and confiscated his estate.

And just like that, Philipsburg Manor vanished. The church and the land now belonged to the state.

Scenes of Desolation

Two years into the war, the farmers' desperation was evident to Rev. Timothy Dwight, D.D., president of Yale College, who lived in Westchester County in 1777. He described what he saw in his book Travels in New-England and New-York:

"Their houses were in a great measure scenes of desolation. Their furniture was extensively plundered or broken to pieces. The walls, floors and windows were injured, both by violence and decay, and were not repaired because they had no means to repair them, and because they were exposed to the repetition of the same injuries. Their cattle were gone. Their enclosures were burnt when they were capable of becoming fuel, and in many cases thrown down when they were not. Their fields were covered with a rank growth of weeds and wild grass."

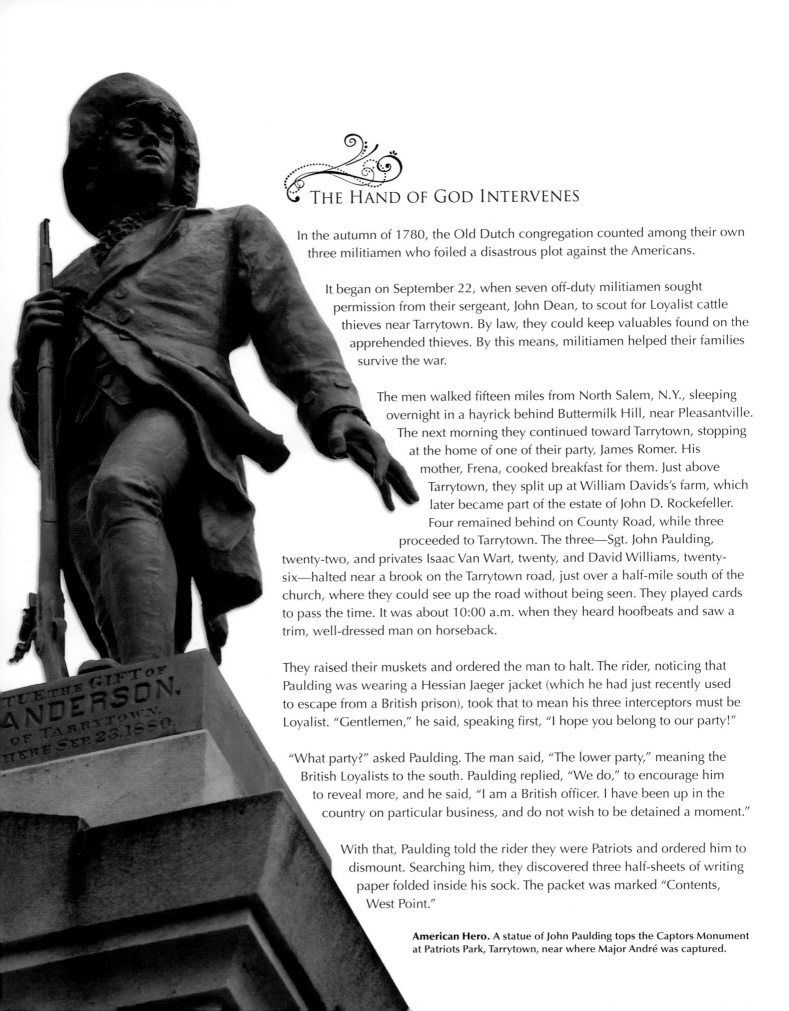

THE HAND OF GOD INTERVENES

In the autumn of 1780, the Old Dutch congregation counted among their own three militiamen who foiled a disastrous plot against the Americans.

It began on September 22, when seven off-duty militiamen sought permission from their sergeant, John Dean, to scout for Loyalist cattle thieves near Tarrytown. By law, they could keep valuables found on the apprehended thieves. By this means, militiamen helped their families survive the war.

The men walked fifteen miles from North Salem, N.Y., sleeping overnight in a hayrick behind Buttermilk Hill, near Pleasantville. The next morning they continued toward Tarrytown, stopping at the home of one of their party, James Romer. His mother, Frena, cooked breakfast for them. Just above Tarrytown, they split up at William Davids's farm, which later became part of the estate of John D. Rockefeller. Four remained behind on County Road, while three proceeded to Tarrytown. The three—Sgt. John Paulding, twenty-two, and privates Isaac Van Wart, twenty, and David Williams, twenty-six—halted near a brook on the Tarrytown road, just over a half-mile south of the church, where they could see up the road without being seen. They played cards to pass the time. It was about 10:00 a.m. when they heard hoofbeats and saw a trim, well-dressed man on horseback.

They raised their muskets and ordered the man to halt. The rider, noticing that Paulding was wearing a Hessian Jaeger jacket (which he had just recently used to escape from a British prison), took that to mean his three interceptors must be Loyalist. "Gentlemen," he said, speaking first, "I hope you belong to our party!"

"What party?" asked Paulding. The man said, "The lower party," meaning the British Loyalists to the south. Paulding replied, "We do," to encourage him to reveal more, and he said, "I am a British officer. I have been up in the country on particular business, and do not wish to be detained a moment."

With that, Paulding told the rider they were Patriots and ordered him to dismount. Searching him, they discovered three half-sheets of writing paper folded inside his sock. The packet was marked "Contents, West Point."

American Hero. A statue of John Paulding tops the Captors Monument at Patriots Park, Tarrytown, near where Major André was captured.

Moment of Truth. André's capture was equal in importance to the surrender at Yorktown.
Illustration: Currier & Ives, courtesy of Library of Congress Prints and Photographs Division.

"He's a spy!" exclaimed Paulding. Rejecting the man's increasingly desperate attempts to bribe them, they headed toward present-day Armonk, N.Y., stopping once more at the Romers' house. As James Romer wrote, "Mom prepared dinner for everyone, but the man refused food. 'Madam,' he kept saying, 'it is all very good, but indeed I cannot eat.'"

At the American army post, the man's identity was soon revealed: Major John André, the adjutant general of the British army. He had met with American general Benedict Arnold, the West Point commander, who had plotted with him to surrender the fort. Arnold had given him the written plans to take back to British headquarters in Manhattan.

When General Washington learned of Arnold's treason, he is said to have burst into tears. Americans had narrowly avoided disaster. Were it not for the young Tarrytown militiamen, the British would have gained control of West Point and the Hudson River, splitting the colonies and most likely leading to the Patriots' defeat. The astonishing event was attributed by many, including Washington, to the hand of God. "The interposition of Providence," Washington called it.

He wrote to Congress, "I do not know the party that took Major André, but it is said that it consisted of only a few militia, who acted in such a manner upon the occasion as does them the highest honor and proves them of great virtue." And later, "They have prevented in all probability our suffering one of the severest strokes that could have been meditated against us."

Congress gave each of the three $1,250, a pension of $200 and a silver medal, presented by General Washington himself. Although the captors were from families associated with the Old Dutch, none of the three are buried there. Paulding is in St. Peter's Churchyard, Peekskill, N.Y.; Williams at Stone Fort, Schoharie County, N.Y.; and Isaac Van Wart in the Old Greenburgh Reformed Churchyard in Elmsford, N.Y. The three are honored by a monument at Patriots Park on Broadway (Route 9) on the Tarrytown/Sleepy Hollow border, where André was captured.

Frena Romer's Bowl

A postscript to the story is recounted by Henry Steiner. "After feeding the men breakfast that fateful morning," he wrote, "Frena Romer prepared lunches for them to take on the road. Some of the food she placed in a pewter bowl in a basket. Later that morning she noticed her pewter bowl was missing. She sent her fifteen-year-old son, John, to fetch it where Paulding, Williams, and Van Wart had forgotten it near André's Brook. In those days a good pewter bowl could be a household treasure."

Lost and Found. This bowl became part of the Major André history. It was handed down in the Romer family from generation to generation and is now at the Tarrytown Historical Society.

Myth or Fact

Romance Nipped in the Bud?

Tradition has it that Mary Philipse, twenty-six, the beautiful, cultured sister of Frederick Philipse III,

Mary Philipse.
Illustration: Historic Hudson Valley.

turned down a marriage proposal from George Washington. Mary met Colonel Washington in February 1756, at the home of a sister, whose husband was Washington's former schoolmate. The story goes that Washington was smitten with Mary and returned for another visit, and asked her to marry him.

Unlikely, says Washington Irving in his biography of Washington. "That he was an open admirer of Miss Philipse is an historical fact," Irving wrote. "That he sought her hand but was refused is not very probable."

Indeed, Washington, commander of the Virginia militia, had little chance to win her affections. In March, a friend in New York warned him "to hasten back before it was too late." British captain Roger Morris was courting her. Washington's duties took him elsewhere, and Morris married her in 1758. In the Revolution, the Morrises fled to England; at one point Washington used their house above the Harlem and Hudson Rivers as his headquarters.

GEORGE WASHINGTON AT THE OLD DUTCH

On July 2, 1781, the tramp of boots and the rumble of artillery and baggage wagons descended on the Old Dutch Church. Down the hill from the north came ranks of marching men, at first by the hundreds, then the thousands, filling up the Albany Post Road. It was not the first time the Old Dutch Church had been witness to large troop movements. Early in the war, in January 1777, a division under General Benjamin Lincoln, taking part in General Washington's strategy against New York, had passed the church on the way to Tarrytown encampments.

Now, several years later, the end of the war was near. How near—and how the Patriots would fare—the weary Continental soldiers did not know. On this midsummer morning, a bystander might have identified the imposing figure of General George Washington himself on horseback at the head of the column. The men had left their encampment at Peekskill at 3:00 a.m. They'd walked eighteen miles, with just one brief stop at the Croton River crossing. As they neared the millworks at Upper Mills, the spreading elms at the Old Dutch Church invited a rest—and perhaps a prayer for his men's safety and a successful campaign. The general ordered a halt at the church until nightfall.

The march resumed, and the army reached Valentine's Hill in Yonkers at sunrise. Meanwhile, other troops were also on the move. General Washington had requested help from the French allies under the command of General Jean-Baptiste de Rochambeau, then in Rhode Island. Now he and his army were closing in on North Castle—today Mount Kisco—to join other American units.

But Washington's move against the British in upper Manhattan was foiled when enemy officers were alerted to the coming attack and withdrew their troops into forts. On July 6 Generals Washington and Rochambeau brought their troops to Ardsley in southern Westchester County. Some 10,000 men set up camp in the Philipsburg hills, while the generals worked on a new strategy.

They were still there in mid-August, when Washington got word of a large

At prayer. George Washington kneeling in his tent, painted by Charles Currier in 1850.
Illustration: Anne S. K. Brown Military Collection, Brown University Library.

Evacuation Day. General Washington proudly rides into New York City, Nov. 25, 1783. Earlier that day, the British embarked for home.
Illustration: Edmund P. Restein, 1879, Library of Congress, Prints and Photographs Division.

French force sailing to Chesapeake Bay. Washington and Rochambeau saw an opening to trap the British encamped on the Yorktown peninsula on the bay. By August 19 the armies were on the move again.

To confuse the enemy in New York City, the Continentals and French took different routes from Ardsley north to the ferry at Verplanck's Point, N.Y., on the Hudson River. For a few days, as Washington Irving put it, all of Westchester County seemed to be alive to the tramp of feet and rolling wheels of the wagons and artillery. Both armies had crossed the Hudson by August 25. By the time they reached Virginia, the French fleet had defeated a British squadron and controlled the Chesapeake. Washington and Rochambeau marshaled their combined forces, now 17,000 strong, and engaged the British in battle. Soon, Lt. Gen. Charles Cornwallis surrendered and 7,000 soldiers were taken prisoner.

Washington next passed by the Old Dutch Church in late 1783. Someone looking out the church window on November 19 of that year would have noticed a few men in blue-and-buff uniforms on horseback—Washington and his staff. This time there were no troops in rapid march, no wagons, no artillery following behind to disturb sleep. This was a happy occasion: The British were leaving New York City.

The men stopped at the Couenhoven Inn in Tarrytown, where they met up with Governor Clinton and Lieutenant Governor Pierre Van Cortlandt. Six days later, on November 25, they were in Manhattan as the British sailed home from New York. Then Washington led 800 Continentals, "ill-clad and weather-beaten," as one onlooker described them, down Broadway. Crowds of New Yorkers cheered wildly.

> " CONVINCED THAT OUR RELIGIOUS LIBERTIES WERE AS ESSENTIAL AS OUR CIVIL, MY ENDEAVORS HAVE NEVER BEEN WANTING TO ENCOURAGE AND PROMOTE THE ONE, WHILE I HAVE BEEN CONTENDING WITH THE OTHER."
>
> — GEORGE WASHINGTON, NOV. 16, 1782, IN A LETTER TO THE KINGSTON, N.Y., REFORMED PROTESTANT DUTCH CHURCH

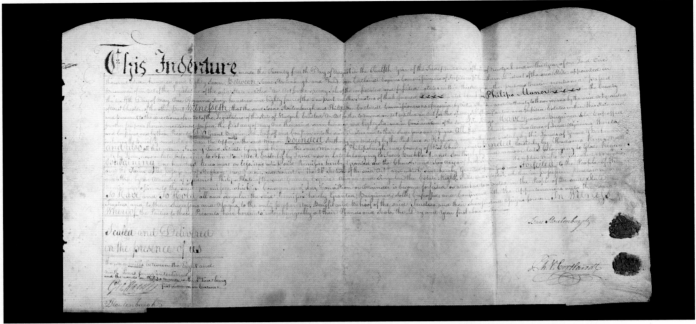

Ownership at Last. The New York State Commissioners of Forfeiture presented this new deed to the trustees of the manor church in 1787.

RINGING OUT WAR

Frederick Philipse III and his family fled to Chester, England. The British government compensated him the enormous sum of £62,075 for his real estate losses. He died in 1785 and was laid to rest in Chester Cathedral, which erected a monument to his memory. The inscription reads in part: "He quitted a province to which he had always been an ornament and benefactor and came to England, leaving all his property behind, which reverse in fortune he bore with that calmness, fortitude and dignity which had distinguished him through every former stage of life."

The congregation wasted no time reopening the church in Sleepy Hollow. The first time they heard the bell must have been a joyous occasion. They removed the lord and lady's "thrones" and replaced the hard oak benches with straight-backed pine pews. In 1785, the church hired its first full-time pastor, Stephen Van Voorhees. Though he shook up the congregation when he baptized Levine Hawes in English—the scandal of it!—from that year on all church records were kept in that language.

Two years later, the confiscated real estate of Frederick Philipse III went on the auction block. Some 300 farms were sold, mostly to the tenant farmers whose families had farmed them for generations. The manor house at Upper Mills was sold to Gerard G. Beekman Jr. and his wife, Cornelia Van Cortlandt, a niece twice-removed of Catherine Philipse. She divided the land nearby into commercial and residential plots. At first she called the new village Beekmantown. Later it was incorporated as North Tarrytown, then renamed Sleepy Hollow in 1996.

The church saw a transformation. The Commissioners of Forfeiture withheld it from auction and in 1787 deeded it and the adjacent burying ground to the deacons and elders to hold in trust for the congregation, which has continued ever since.

Patriots in the Burying Ground

October 19, 1894, started with a bang, as a twenty-one-gun salute boomed across a cloudless sky over Tarrytown. The honors to mark the dedication of a Revolutionary War monument were done by two navy warships anchored in the river and the artillery batteries camped nearby. By 10:00 a.m., thousands of spectators had lined up to watch a military parade. The parade ended at Battle Hill in Sleepy Hollow Cemetery, which overlooks the Old Dutch Burying Ground. Spectators gathered around a flag-draped monument near a Revolutionary War lunette, an earthwork in the shape of a half-moon. During the war, local Patriots had built the lunette; from there a battery of cannons kept watch on the Albany Post Road where it crossed the Pocantico bridge.

Battle Hill Monument. Dedicated in 1894, the granite monument, just north of the church, lists the names of 76 Revolutionary soldiers buried in the churchyard.

The monument lists the names of seventy-six Revolutionary soldiers buried in the Old Dutch churchyard. (At least one, Samuel Youngs, has since been moved to another cemetery.) The last veteran of that war was laid to rest in the Burying Ground in November 1851. At the 1894 dedication ceremony, Judge Isaac N. Mills noted that nowhere in the state are the graves of the Revolutionary heroes to be "locally held in more tender regard than right here in ancient Sleepy Hollow." He continued:

> *They were noble men, though plain, common folk. Their character was simple, massive and rugged. The free air of these hills taught them the rights of man far better than their manorial master learned the same in schools and legislative councils. They knew by instinct at least that governments derive their just powers from the "consent of the governed," and that there is no such thing as "the divine right of kings to rule."*

> *The Declaration of Independence with its grand statement of the right of self-government … fell upon their eager ears and went to their responsive hearts as a benediction of heaven-born truth. Much as they respected and loved their landlord, Frederick Philipse, knowing as they did his pure personal character and upright life, yet even his vast personal influence was impotent to change their views or swerve them from what they deemed to be their duty.*

> " HE WILL JUDGE BETWEEN THE NATIONS AND WILL SETTLE DISPUTES FOR MANY PEOPLES. THEY WILL BEAT THEIR SWORDS INTO PLOWSHARES AND THEIR SPEARS INTO PRUNING HOOKS. NATION WILL NOT TAKE UP SWORD AGAINST NATION, NOR WILL THEY TRAIN FOR WAR ANYMORE."
>
> —ISAIAH 2:4

Locals in the Thick of the Fight

There are many heroic tales to be told about the farmer-Patriots of Philipsburg. Both men and women took up arms to defend their families and farms and defeat the British. Seventy-six Revolutionary soldiers were buried in the Old Dutch Burying Ground; many more did their part. Here are just a few of their stories.

Motif for a 1926 commemorative stamp, "The Battle of White Plains." Illustration: Courtesy of the White Plains Public Library

Here Be Heroes. Revolutionary soldiers' graves are marked by a plaque and flag.

Epitaph

Jacob Van Tassel's simple headstone, now too eroded to read, records that he died August 24, 1840, age 95 years, 11 months and 22 days.

The simple stone points to the honorable grave,

Where sleeps the Patriot pure, the Soldier brave,

Reader, if to thy heart thy country's cause be dear,

His service call to mind; this grave revere.

Jacob Van Tassel — *Hero with the Goose Gun*

The name Van Tassel was as common in the colony as Smith or Jones is today. The name means "of Texel," an island off the Dutch coast. Jacob Van Tassel (d. 1840) and his cousins Cornelius (d. 1820) and Petrus (d. 1784) were church members and Patriots. Jacob farmed 185 acres along the Hudson, including the riverside homestead of early settler Wolfert Ecker. During the war, Jacob would scout from the riverbank for British boats on the Hudson. Washington Irving told Jacob's story in "Wolfert's Roost"—it was confirmed in Jacob's April 1836 pension application.

> The stout Jacob was not idle; he was prone to carry on a petty warfare of his own.... Did he ever chance to espy, from his look-out place, a hostile ship or galley anchored or becalmed near shore, he would take down his long goose-gun from the hooks over the fireplace, sally out alone, and lurk along shore, dodging behind rocks and trees and watching for hours.... As a boat came within shot, bang! went the great goose-gun; a shower of slugs and buckshot whistled about the ears of the enemy, and before the boat could reach the shore, Jacob had scuttled up some woody ravine, and left no trace behind.

The British captured Jacob and his scouting party, burned his home and imprisoned him. (See Chapter 6 for Irving's perhaps-fanciful story about the attempted kidnapping of Jacob's daughter Eleanor.)

After the war, Jacob Van Tassel bought the land he'd farmed and rebuilt his house. In 1802, it passed to Captain Oliver Ferris, whose son, Benson, sold it to Washington Irving in 1835. He enlarged and renovated the home and named it Sunnyside.

Solemn March. The 7th Massachusetts Regiment, which served most of the war in the Hudson Valley, reenacts a funeral at New Windsor, N.Y., Cantonment.

Petrus and Cornelius Van Tassel

The Cousins

After British troop excursions against Peekskill and Tarrytown fell short of success in 1777, Royalist governor William Tryon's solution was to burn Tarrytown or, at least, parts of it. On the cold night of November 17, 1777, he sent allied Hessian (German) troops to burn several homes east of the hamlet. Cornelius Van Tassel and his cousin Petrus, militia officers who lived on adjoining farms east of Tarrytown, were among those targeted. Harsh and mean-spirited Major Andreas Emmerick led the attack, dismounting in Cornelius's barnyard and shouting at the occupants to surrender. Instead, the Van Tassels opened fire.

"The houses are owned by damned Rebels," Emmerick yelled furiously. "Burn them!"

His soldiers looted and torched Cornelius's house, forcing the family outside after stripping them of warm clothes. Cornelius's wife, Elizabeth, suddenly realized their baby Leah was missing. Flames shot from the house. Elizabeth raced back to search for her child but collapsed in tears at the door. She saw a young Hessian soldier motion for her to follow him. Behind a shed was Leah, safe and warm in a blanket. Elizabeth and her baby hid in a dirt cellar until it was safe to seek shelter. As for Cornelius and cousin Petrus, they were captured and imprisoned for nearly a year.

Luck or Destiny?

While still a teenager, John Dean (d. 1817) and his brother William were among the first from the manor to join the Patriot cause, going to Canada in the Campaign of 1775 to fight in Quebec. William died— probably from smallpox—and John, sick, suffering and without money, made his way home, carrying his brother's watch and silver sleeve buttons.

After the Battle of White Plains in 1776, John had recovered enough to enlist as a sergeant in the militia and fight in local skirmishes. In September 1780, to ward off Tory pillaging of local farms, he sent seven militiamen to scout the roads near Tarrytown. Three of them apprehended British spy Major John André, who was carrying Benedict Arnold's maps of the fort at West Point. The rest, as they say, is history.

73

The Martlings

The Liberty Boys

Daring Exploit. Abraham Martling, the son, led a dangerous raid into the British camp.

The Patriarch. Abraham Martling is called Tarrytown's founding father.

Isaac the Martyr. "Inhumanely slain."

The November 1777 raids on two Van Tassel farms angered locals. Abraham Martling (d. 1786), a daredevil whose exploits against the enemy gained him fame, met with some Tarrytown men at a tavern to plot "a stroke of vengeance worthy of one of Homer's heroes" for its boldness of conception, according to one published report.

On the evening of November 25, Martling, a boatman by occupation, led a band of young blades on a wildly daring raid to Manhattan Island, right into the heart of the British camp. In two light whaleboats shaped like canoes, Martling and his men made their way secretly down the Hudson. They slipped past the Water Guard, scaled the rugged heights of Bloomingdale and then pillaged and set fire to the fine home of General Oliver Delancey, a leading Loyalist and the lieutenant governor's brother. The band of men returned home safely.

Like the Van Tassels, the Martlings were members of the Old Dutch Church. The patriarch was Abraham Martling (d. 1761), a blacksmith and a deacon. He used the Dutch spelling of his name, Martlenghs, and his headstone is in Dutch, so presumably he spoke Dutch in his day-to-day life. Though the English had gained control of New Netherland in 1664 and renamed it New York, English did not become the predominant language among the Philipsburg Manor Dutch until around 1800. The elder Martling could be called Tarrytown's founding father. Upon his death his farm was divided into lots and developed into what became the village of Tarrytown.

Another son of the elder Martling was Isaac (d. 1779), who after his death became known as Isaac the Martyr. He was the manor's first murder victim. Until the headstone broke off years ago, it was a local attraction for visitors. The stone, carved by Solomon Brewer, bore these words: "Inhumanely slain by Nathaniel Underhill, May 26, 1779."

What happened? Some historians write that Martling had once caused Underhill's arrest. *Tales of the Old Dutch Burying Ground* tells a different story: Revolutionary times saw sickness and hunger throughout Westchester County. Only one resident appeared to prosper: Nathaniel Underhill, who made no apologies for his British sympathies.... No grain was ever given to his unfortunate neighbors. One day Isaac, a one-armed veteran of the French and Indian War, led an angry mob to Underhill's home. They dragged the Loyalist to his barn and strung him by his heels from a crossbeam.

Underhill plotted revenge. One day when Martling was heading to a stream to fetch water, Underhill pulled his sword and mortally wounded Isaac. Never seen again in Tarrytown, Underhill likely fled to Nova Scotia and lived among Tory sympathizers.

Edward and Ann Couenhoven

The Tavern Keeper's Family

Taverns are lively gathering places for food, fellowship and news of the day. Edward Couenhoven (d. 1786) ran the celebrated Couenhoven Inn, located at the northwest corner of Main Street and Broadway in Tarrytown. His eatery was famous for its excellent hospitality and welcomed many a Revolutionary leader, including George Washington. Edward was a member of Colonel Hammond's regiment. When he was called to duty, his good *vrouw,* Ann (d. 1797), ably ran the inn … and conducted a little espionage at the same time.

Concealed on the side of the tavern's fireplace was an "auditory pipe," or small box, that went to the floor above. This eavesdropping device helped the Couenhovens obtain information on enemy military maneuvers—so no wonder Washington stopped by.

The story is told that during one of George Washington's visits to the tavern, he took the Couenhovens' daughter Ann, then a little girl, onto his knee and kissed her. After the Revolution ended, town fathers chose this tavern as the location to auction off parcels of the confiscated Philipsburg Manor.

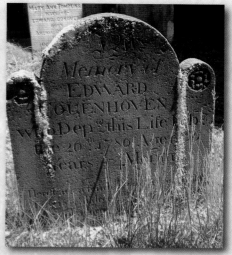

The Innkeeper. This simple sandstone marker belongs to the patriarch of the Couenhoven family, Edward. During the war, he ran an inn.

William Davids

Prominent Patriot

Reenacting History. A Continental soldier begins the process of loading his musket.

William Davids (d. 1787) was a church member and an elder, justice of the peace, town supervisor and a tenant of Philipsburg Manor. He farmed a hillside called Davids Hill. On April 13, 1775, at the request of his landlord, then Frederick Philipse III, William Davids's name appears on a petition that protested "unlawful congresses and committees" and pledged support to the king. But, unlike Philipse, Davids would break with the Crown. By 1776 Davids had became a leading Patriot and member of the Committee of Safety.

Davids's house earned a place in Revolutionary history when George Washington rode there in 1776 before the Battle of White Plains to consult Lieutenant Colonel Hammond about the military situation in the Tarrytown area. Washington visited again after the Battle of White Plains. The house no longer stands, but its doorposts were said to have taken several saber slashes made out of frustration by British soldiers who arrived one day expecting to find General Washington, who'd left already. The militiamen who captured Major André stopped here before spotting the spy.

Davids Hill was purchased in 1893 by John D. Rockefeller Sr.

Westchester Guides

The Westchester Guides were an elite group chosen for their knowledge of the roads and the country. Among them was Lieutenant John Odell (d. 1835), son of Patriot and church member Jonathan Odell (d. 1818). Lieutenant Odell himself was singled out by the British, who offered £100 for his capture.

Shortly before the end of the war, Lieutenant Odell and Captain Daniel Williams attempted to capture the notorious Colonel James Delancey, the former Westchester County sheriff whose "cowboys" were a nasty band of marauders.

On January 24, 1783, Williams and Odell led fifty horsemen from Peekskill, northern Westchester County, down the Albany Post Road past the Old Dutch Church to Dobbs Ferry, then east through Eastchester to West Farms to Delancey's heavily guarded house in Morrisania (today the South Bronx). They arrived at midnight and failed to find Delancey, who was hiding in the pigpen. Instead they took two prisoners, fifteen horses and valuables in the house. Pursued by the enemy, they hurriedly retraced their route up the Albany Post Road past the church. Feeling safe, they stopped in Ossining to divide up the loot.

The hundred enemy horsemen in pursuit had not given up. Their devastating attack on the Americans left one dead and several wounded. They captured fifteen, including John Paulding, a captor of Major André.

War Hero. Joseph and Susannah Youngs's grave marker is in the foreground.

Joseph Youngs

Justice of the Peace

Joseph Youngs (d. 1789) was a "man of consequence" from a prominent family on the manor. During the war, he was a militia member, justice of the peace and a member of the Committee of Safety. One of his duties was to keep General Washington informed of British maneuvers. Youngs's farm lay just inside American lines four miles east of the church. American officers gathered there to plot strategy. Important officers such as General Tadeusz Kosciusko and Colonel Aaron Burr were stationed there. This made his farm a ripe target for British raids.

The British decided to rid themselves of Youngs and his activities for good. In early 1780, 100 horsemen and 500 infantry set out at night on a twenty-mile march north from Manhattan, hoping to arrive at the farm undetected. Deep snow on the ground slowed their progress, and the march took all night. Next morning the attack began. Some 250 Continental troops put up a fierce defense and the battle lasted most of the day. When it was over, thirteen Americans were dead, seventeen were wounded, and ninety were marched off to prison in New York City. Youngs's house and outbuildings were burned to the ground. Youngs survived the assault and died nine years later.

For years afterward, the farmer who bought the land after the war would occasionally turn up a bone or other evidence of human remains while plowing.

CHAPTER 6

"The Legend" and
the Church
That Inspired It

Washington Irving put the Old Dutch Church on the world map when he published "The Legend of Sleepy Hollow." Coming from a young nation without a tradition of storytelling, Irving was hailed as the Founding Father of American Literature. His "Legend" became America's best-loved ghost story, creating in legions of readers a fascination with the little church whose "whitewashed walls shine modestly forth, like Christian purity." How did he choose the church? Who were his characters? What's so spooky about the ride of the Headless Horseman? There's spine-tingling evidence ...

On the Run! William J. Wilgus's *Ichabod Crane, Respectfully Dedicated to Washington Irving,* 1856, is one of many depictions of the Headless Horseman.
Illustrations: Historic Hudson Valley. Page 77 detail, *The Headless Horseman Pursuing Ichabod Crane,* John Quidor, 1858. Smithsonian American Art Museum.

WASHINGTON IRVING: PUTTING "OLD DUTCH" ON THE WORLD MAP

Rising at midnight. Ringing the church bell. Jumping over gravestones. Other boyish pranks ... That's how in 1798 Washington Irving, then a mere teenager, embraced his first summer in Tarrytown, N.Y. Rev. James Selden Spencer, once rector of Christ Episcopal Church, called that summer to mind:

> *Think of the innate love of fun which prompted Washington Irving, when a boy on a visit to General Paulding's house in this village, to rise at midnight, go up to the Old Dutch Church and there energetically ring the church bell to the alarm of all the ghost-fearing burghers round the country, and you have the germ of that mirth-provoking spirit, which diffused cheerfulness and good humor all around him.*

And from those bucolic days, the soon-to-be celebrated storyteller would embark on his own legendary career.

Irving was born on April 3, 1783, into a relatively peaceful period in our country's history, and died in 1859. His life was bookended by two wars: the Revolutionary War and the Civil War. A New Yorker, the last of eleven children in a Scottish-English family, he was named after his parents' hero, General George Washington.

Once as a young boy, the story goes, his old Scottish nurse held him up so he could see George Washington in a public procession. But that wasn't sufficient. The next day she spotted him in a shop along Broadway. "Please, Your Excellency," she said, "here's a bairn that's called after ye!" General Washington turned and gave his blessing.

As a fifteen-year-old Irving got his first real taste of quaint Dutch customs. An outbreak of yellow fever was sweeping Manhattan. So the teenager was sent upriver to Tarrytown to spend the summer with his brother William and his wife, Julia Paulding, whose family was half-Dutch ("Pauldinck" was the original name). Her brother James K. Paulding became a lifelong friend.

Washington Meets Washington. *The Chieftain and the Child,* 1854, by George B. Butler, captures the fateful meeting. Illustration: Historic Hudson Valley.

Self-Portrait. Washingon Irving in 1851.

(William, James and Washington eventually collaborated on *Salmagundi*, a monthly literary magazine containing good-humored sallies about the foibles of the day. And the Pauldings' cousin John was among the captors of Major André during the Revolutionary War.)

During carefree days the teen paddled in the Pocantico, soaked up quaint Dutch folklore and wandered among the old headstones in the Old Dutch Burying Ground. The church, as Irving explained, was the "only place of worship for a wide neighborhood." The Pauldings were long-standing members, so young Irving attended Sunday services with them and squirmed under the church elders' "stern" and "vigilant" regard, as recorded in his essay "Sleepy Hollow," published in *Knickerbocker* magazine, 1839:

> *Around the pulpit sat the elders of the church, reverend, gray-headed, leathern-visaged men, whom I regarded with awe, as so many apostles. They were stern in their sanctity, kept a vigilant eye upon my giggling companions and myself, and shook a rebuking finger at any boyish device to relieve the tediousness of compulsory devotion.*

Later as a young writer living in London, Irving distilled his childhood memories of this area and the church into the setting for "The Legend of Sleepy Hollow." It was one of a series of essays and stories for a book, *The Sketch Book of Geoffrey Crayon, Gent.* At the time, Irving was worrying over the

On the Waterfront. This painting, showing activity in 1810 along New York's Hudson River, is by Baroness Hyde de Neuville. Illustration: New-York Historical Society.

Bon Voyage!

"Sailing up [the Hudson] was like going to Europe, and friends and relatives assembled on the wharf to speed the adventurous voyager with handkerchiefs and tears. On board the long days lent themselves to storytelling. The Hudson River sloops, in one of which Irving sailed, carried furs from Albany, and every river town had sloops of its own to convey the local produce to the New York market. They were sometimes as long as seventy feet and painted like Italian carts, with gay stripes of gold, red, green and blue, and were stowed with chicken-coops and boxes and often with carriages and horses."

—*Van Wyck Brooks,* The World of Washington Irving, *1944*

Something in the Air

"Whether 'Legend of Sleepy Hollow' is a pure creation of the great writer, or whether he grasped at something that was in the air we may not be able to say, but it is an unforgettable story, and is linked in with the Old Church. It was over the bridge that spans the stream that sweeps about the church that the Headless Horseman desperately rode when he threw his head at the terrified schoolmaster on that awful night; it was in the church that Ichabod Crane led the singing, and we recall the picture sketched by that wizard of the pen of the little building on its knoll.... Sleepy Hollow was the creation of Irving, and the name Old Dutch Church of Sleepy Hollow would never have been applied if it were not for him."

—*Reverend John Knox Allen, pastor emeritus, Old Dutch Church, 1928*

bankruptcy of his family's trading business in England. According to a 1983 article in *Smithsonian*, "a therapeutic dose of literary composition seemed advisable" to draw him out of a "melancholy that corroded his spirits and rusted all the springs of mental energy."

On March 3, 1819, in sending the first essays in *The Sketch Book* to his brother Ebenezer in New York, "babblings fit only for a brother's eye," he confided:

> *My spirits are very unequal, and my mind depends upon them; and I am easily thrown into such a state of perplexity and such depression as to incapacitate me for any mental exertion. Do not, I beseech you, impute my lingering in Europe to any indifference to my own country or my friends. My greatest desire is to make myself worthy of the good-will of my country, and my greatest anticipation of happiness is the return to my friends. I am living here in a retired and solitary way, and partaking in little of the gaiety of life, but I am determined not to return home until I have sent some writings before me that shall, if they have merit, make me return to the smiles, rather than skulk back to the pity, of my friends.*

Irving sent his brother a sixth installment on December 29. "There is a Knickerbocker story that may please from its representation of American scenes," he wrote. "It is a random thing suggested by recollections of scenes and stories around Tarrytown. The story is a mere whimsical band to connect descriptions of scenery, customs, manners, etc." It was "The Legend of Sleepy Hollow."

Irving's nephew and biographer, Pierre Munroe Irving, explained in *The Life and Letters of Washington Irving* that the outlines for the story were written about a year earlier in Birmingham, England, after his sister's husband talked about growing up in Tarrytown. The sketch "touched upon a waggish fiction of one Brom Bones, a wild blade, who professed to fear nothing, and boasted of his having once met the devil on a return from a nocturnal frolic, and run a race with him for a bowl of milk-punch," explained Pierre Irving. "The imagination of the author suddenly kindled over the recital, and in a few hours he scribbled off the framework of his renowned story and was reading it aloud. He then threw it by until he went to London, where it was expanded into the present legend."

"The Legend of Sleepy Hollow" and the other pieces in *The Sketch Book*, including "Rip Van Winkle," appeared between 1819 and 1820, first in the United States and then in England. They were an immediate success on both continents. The colorful characters in "The Legend"—the awkward and superstitious schoolteacher Ichabod Crane, who sang in the church choir and courted country belle Katrina Van Tassel; the Headless Horseman, who "tethered his horse nightly among the graves in the church yard" and, yes, Katrina's other suitor, the "burly, roaring, roystering blade" Brom Bones—have spooked and enchanted literally millions of readers ever since.

Historic Page.
The opening paragraphs of "The Legend of Sleepy Hollow" show Irving's corrections to his riveting ghost story. His portrait, painted in 1820 by Charles Robert Leslie (courtesy of Historic Hudson Valley), was made the same year Irving finished writing "The Legend."

Sunday Morning in Sleepy Hollow. Worshippers gather at the Old Dutch in this painting by Jennie Brownscombe (late 19th century).

Glory Be to God on High

In a memorial discourse, Rev. William Creighton, Irving's pastor at Christ Episcopal Church, talked about his religious life: "One Sabbath morning he approached me," said Rev. Creighton, "and asked why we could not have the 'Gloria in Excelsis' sung every Sunday. I replied that I had no objection, and that there was nothing whatever to prevent it; and at the same time inquired of him, 'Do you like it?'

"'Like it? Like it?' said he. 'Above all things. Why, it contains the sum and substance of our faith; and I never hear it without feeling better, and without my heart being lifted up.'"

"The church gains an added charm," acknowledged the church fathers at its 200th anniversary celebration, "because the pen of Irving has cast a halo of romance about it." In turn, the Old Dutch Church of Sleepy Hollow has become a cherished icon worldwide.

The Founding Father of American Literature, as Irving became known, was also a statesman, poet and historian. He wrote a wide range of scholarly works. He compiled books on Christopher Columbus; the Moorish palace of the Alhambra in Spain; and business tycoon John Jacob Astor's fur-trading adventures—and not to be overlooked is his five-volume biography of George Washington.

In an article on Irving, Joseph T. Butler, Historic Hudson Valley's first curator, recalls some of the author's many other distinctions:

> *Spain elected Irving to membership in the Real Academia de la Historia (1828) and England's Royal Society of Literature voted him its prized Gold Medal in History (1830). He declined an offer from the Tammany Society to run for Mayor of the City of New York in 1838, but he did serve for ten years as the first president of the Astor Library, forerunner of the New York Public Library. In 1849 the Smithsonian Institution elected Irving an honorary member in that prestigious organization.*

"There was no man in the early years of our Republic who did more than this man to arouse good will towards America," said writer Edgar Mayhew Bacon in summing up Irving's contributions. "Not only was he America's favorite son overseas, but he was a favorite son in America ... He was respected in all parts

82

of the country and by all parties. Presidents consulted him, and behind the curtain he gave quiet advice which, at critical times, help to avert war between America and England, and between America and France."

What do we learn of Tarrytown from the worldly Irving? For one thing, he delighted in an imaginative description of how the village may have been named. "The name of Tarry Town," he wrote in the "The Legend of Sleepy Hollow," was given "by the good housewives of the adjacent country from the inveterate propensity of their husbands to linger about the village tavern on market days."

We also learn what Sleepy Hollow meant to Irving. He was the first to call the community by that name. Here's what he says in "The Legend":

> There is a little valley among high hills, which is one of the quietest places in the whole world. A small brook glides through it, with just murmur enough to lull one to repose, and the occasional whistle of a quail or tapping of a woodpecker.... If ever I should wish for a retreat whither I might steal from the world and its distractions and dream quietly away the remnant of a troubled life, I know of none more promising than this little valley.

Irving did in fact spend the latter years of his life nearby. In 1835, after living for seventeen years in Europe, he purchased a "neglected cottage" close by the Hudson River in Tarrytown that became his beloved home, Sunnyside. Soon Irving embellished the original farmhouse and turned it into a "little old-fashioned stone mansion, all made up of gabled-ends, and as full of angles and corners as an old cocked hat." This home was, he wrote, "a beautiful spot, capable of being made a little paradise." He attended Christ Episcopal Church in Tarrytown, where he served as a warden.

For the rest of his life, Irving lived at Sunnyside except for four years in the 1840s, when he was called away to become minister to Spain. That country's political unrest left him homesick and disheartened. Irving yearned for the time, as he wrote, in "my literary career when poor as a rat, but rich in dreams, I beheld the world through the medium of my imagination and was apt to believe men as good as I wished them to be."

Irving never married (his fiancée, Matilda, died in 1809 and he is said to have carried a lovely miniature of her and a locket of her fair hair for the rest of his life). He shared Sunnyside with his brother Ebenezer and his five daughters. And there's something quite remarkable about Washington Irving's own last chapter. Just eight months before his death, he completed *The Life of George Washington*—a tribute to his namesake. On the eve of the Civil War, on November 28, 1859, the writer died peacefully at home.

Washington Irving's final resting place is but a short walk up the hill from the Old Dutch Church, in the adjoining Sleepy Hollow Cemetery. The grave is marked by a simple marble headstone with a rounded top. Fittingly, it overlooks the church he made world-famous.

Myth or Fact

Did Irving Attend the Old Dutch?

Alas, no. While Irving visited the Old Dutch Church, first as a teenager wandering through the graveyard and later as an adult, he actually became a member of Tarrytown's Christ Episcopal Church, founded in 1837. After he joined in 1848, he became a communicant and warden, and was generous with donations: the organ, the heating plant and even the ivy that covered the tower; the ivy clippings were given to him by Sir Walter Scott, transplanted from his home in Abbotsford, Scotland.

When people came to the church and asked to see Irving, members of the vestry are reported to have said, "Wait until the offering is taken and you will see him passing among the people with the plate." One Sunday after church Irving remarked: "I have passed that plate so often up and down the aisle that I begin to feel like a highwayman. I feel as if I could stop a man on the road, and say, 'Your money, or your life.'"

Life Along the Hudson. This fanciful depiction of Washington Irving's home Sunnyside, circa 1860, is by an unknown artist. Said Irving of his home, "Though but of small dimension, yet like many small people, it is of mighty spirit." Illustration: Historic Hudson Valley.

A Tarrytown Farewell

"When Washington Irving died at the age of seventy-six, New York City went into mourning," wrote Sleepy Hollow historian Henry Steiner in the *River Journal*. "Flags throughout the city were hung at half-mast, banks closed for a day and hordes of people traveled to Tarrytown on December 1, 1859, to attend the funeral. On a warm, Indian summer day, nearly a thousand people who could not fit into Christ Church crowded outside the door. A procession of 150 carriages escorted the body to Sleepy Hollow Cemetery." In 1968, a local newspaper article, "Thousands Attended Tarrytown Funeral of Irving," recapped what happened next:

> *The funeral route passed through the very scenes that the pen of Mr. Irving had rendered.... At the Old Dutch Church the carriages drew to a halt, except for those carrying family members and church dignitaries. These few carriages continued on up a grassy mount which Irving had described*

Nom de Plume. This sketch of Diedrich Knickerbocker (aka Washington Irving), the crusty Dutch narrator of *A History of New York* and "The Legend of Sleepy Hollow," was by illustrator Felix O. C. Darley, 1849.

as "the burying ground where families are garnered together, side by side, in long platoons, in this last gathering place of kindred."

Atop this mount lay the Irving family plot, chosen by Irving himself a week before his death. The coffin was lowered beneath a large oak. Historian George Bancroft wrote, "No American since President George Washington has taken to the grave the undivided affection of the American people like Irving."

After Irving's death, poet Henry Wadsworth Longfellow told members of the Massachusetts Historical Society: "Every reader has his first book; I mean to say, one book among all others which in early youth first fascinates his imagination, and at once excites and satisfies the desires of his mind. To me, this first book was the *Sketch Book* of Washington Irving." At the same gathering Longfellow saluted Irving's formidable role in promoting American literature. "We feel a just pride in his renown as an author," he said, "not forgetting that, to his other claims upon our gratitude, he adds also that of having been the first to win for our country an honourable name and position in the History of Letters."

Final Resting Place

Washington Irving considered having a family vault or burying ground established at the Old Dutch Church, as indicated in a letter dated 1842 to his brother Ebenezer. In this most-cherished area, he said, "I hope, some day or other, to sleep my last sleep in that favorite resort of my boyhood."

Instead, he eventually settled on Sleepy Hollow Cemetery, which incorporated in 1849. "I send you herewith a plan of a rural cemetery projected by some of the worthies of Tarrytown, on the woody hills adjacent to the Sleepy Hollow Church," he wrote in 1849 to Gaylord Clark, then editor of Knickerbocker magazine. "I have no pecuniary interest in it, yet I hope it may succeed, as it will keep that beautiful and umbrageous neighbourhood sacred from the anti-poetical and all-leveling ax. Besides, I trust that I shall one day lay my bones there."

In the Churchyard at Tarrytown

Beloved Storyteller. Two earlier gravestones were chipped away by eager tourists, so the replacement was rounded. Photo: Jim Logan.

Here lies the gentle humorist, who died
In the bright Indian Summer of his fame
A simple stone, with but a date and name,
Marks his secluded resting-place beside
The river that he loved and glorified.
Here in the autumn of his days he came,
But the dry leaves of life were all aflame
With tints that brightened and were multiplied.
How sweet a life was his; how sweet a death!
Living, to wing with mirth the weary hours,
Or with romantic tales the heart to cheer;
Dying, to leave a memory like the breath
Of summers full of sunshine and of showers,
A grief and gladness in the atmosphere.

—Henry Wadsworth Longfellow

Haunt of the Headless Horseman. At night, the light from a nearby street lamp casts an eerie glow over the Burying Ground.

Quintessential American Place

"Washington Irving shows us Sleepy Hollow as he witnessed it, still connected with its colonial past and Dutch ways, a place living peacefully in agrarian seclusion, a decade or two after the momentous conflict of the American Revolution. It is a society of common folk, as yet untouched by the great wave of enterprise and change, which is beginning to sweep the infant nation."

—Henry Steiner, Sleepy Hollow village historian

AMERICA'S BEST-LOVED GHOST STORY

As for the characters in "The Legend of Sleepy Hollow," what's true, what's not? For those dying to know more, look over your shoulder, watch your back. Ghosts from the Old Dutch Church and Burying Ground await you ... Who were these unforgettable characters and where did Irving encounter them? Only Washington Irving knows for sure. Remember, even Diedrich Knickerbocker, the nom de plume Irving used for his storyteller, is questioned that his tale seems "a little on the extravagant." His reply: "As to that matter, I don't believe one-half of it myself."

The Headless Horseman: His Tale Is Still Around

"The Legend" says: "The dominant spirit, however, that haunts this enchanted region, and seems to be commander-in-chief of all the powers of the air, is the apparition of a figure on horseback without a head."

What better way to learn about the Headless Horseman than to listen to Geoffrey Crayon himself, the storyteller in Irving's ghost story? Here is his description of the Hessian soldier whose head was shot off by a cannon: "The apparition is said by some to be the ghost of a Hessian trooper, whose head had been carried away by a cannon ball, in some nameless battle during the Revolutionary War.... His haunts are not confined to the valley, but extend at times to the vicinity of a church at no great distance. Indeed, certain historians

Daydreaming Schoolmaster. This and the other illustrations on pages 86–90 were created in 1849 by Philadelphia-born artist Felix O. C. Darley. All Darley illustrations: Historic Hudson Valley.

who have been careful in collecting and collating the floating facts concerning this specter allege that the body of the trooper has been buried in the churchyard."

Alas, Irving never mentioned the location of the Headless Horseman's grave. A few years ago a sexton thought to correct Irving's lapse. He placed a small grave marker for the Horseman in an open spot behind the church, only to have it disappear soon after. He replaced it with another marker. It also vanished. With that, he gave up. It appears the "souvenir" was just too tempting to "Legend" fans!

Katrina Van Tassel: The Country Coquette

"The Legend" says: "The daughter and only child of a substantial Dutch farmer. She was a blooming lass of fresh eighteen; plump as a partridge; ripe and melting and rosy-cheeked as one of her father's peaches."

Who was the inspiration for the flirty belle in "The Legend" who set her admirers by the ears with her coquetries? The delectable Katrina, with a "provokingly short petticoat, to display the prettiest foot and ankle in the country round"? Most historians look to Eleanor Van Tassel Brush (died 1861, age ninety-eight) who was a young woman when Washington Irving visited Tarrytown as a teen in 1798. Her elaborate marble monument is in the Old Dutch Burying Ground. Both she and Katrina shared the same last name and Irving included the story of Eleanor's near-abduction in "Wolfert's Roost." And that's not all: in 1835, he purchased what was once the Van Tassel family farm on the Hudson and renamed it Sunnyside.

Was she truly his inspiration? Irving never revealed his sources, but he could have met Eleanor. Or as a teen he might have wandered in the Old Dutch Burying Ground past the elaborately carved headstone of Catriena Ecker Van Tassel (died 1793, age fifty-six) and chosen variant spellings of this charming Dutch name. But the mystery still swirls in the mists of time, because our famous storyteller is said to have also hinted coyly to several local ladies that they were his "Katrina."

The Abduction of Eleanor Van Tassel (aka Katrina)

Irving gave this fanciful description of Eleanor Van Tassel's near-abduction in "Wolfert's Roost," written in 1855. Her father, Jacob, was away with a scouting party during the Revolutionary War when a boat full of British troops stormed their farm. Only her mother, aunt Nochie and Dinah, a house servant, were at home. They, a "garrison" of only a few women, made a vociferous outcry and defended themselves:

The garrison flew to arms, that is to say, to mops, broom-sticks, shovels, tongs, and all kinds of domestic weapons; for, unluckily, the great piece of ordnance, the goose-gun, was absent with its owner. Above all, a vigorous defense was made with that most potent of female weapons, the tongue. Never did invaded hen-roost make a more vociferous outcry. The house was sacked and plundered, fire was set, and in a few moments its blaze shed a baleful light far over the Tappan Sea.

Then, what horror, one of the soldiers grabbed Eleanor and endeavored to carry her off to the boat, and here began a tug-of-war. Mother, Auntie and Dinah flew to her rescue. Irving picks up with what happened: "The struggle continued down to the very water's edge" until "a voice from the armed vessel at anchor ordered the spoilers to let go their hold; they relinquished their prize, jumped into their boats, and pulled off, and the heroine of the Roost escaped with a mere rumpling of the feathers."

Leisure Time

"The sage inhabitants of Sleepy Hollow had read in their Bible, which was the only book they studied, that labor was originally inflicted upon man as a punishment of sin.... Was anyone compelled, by dire necessity, to repair his house, mend his fences, build a barn, or get in a harvest, he considered it a great evil that entitled him to call in the assistance of his friends. He

accordingly proclaimed a 'bee,' or rustic gathering; whereupon all his neighbors hurried to his aid, like faithful allies; attacked the task with the desperate energy of lazy men, eager to overcome a job; and when it was accomplished, fell to eating and drinking, fiddling and dancing, for very joy that so great an amount of labor had been vanquished, with so little sweating of the brow."

—WASHINGTON IRVING
"SLEEPY HOLLOW,"
KNICKERBOCKER, 1839

Baltus Van Tassel, Contented Farmer

"The Legend" says: "A thriving, contented, liberal-hearted farmer. Everything was snug, happy and well-conditioned."

Not much evidence exists for the model for Baltus Van Tassel. Could it be someone with a similar last name such as John Van Tassel (died 1807, age sixty-nine)? Rotund, a mere five-foot, six-inches tall, Van Tassel was a laborer and served during the Revolutionary War. He was the proprietor of the Van Tassel Inn (later called the Mott House). Young Irving could have encountered Van Tassel in Tarrytown.

As an adult, Irving had a well-documented connection to the inn, then owned by the Motts, where his sister stayed. In *Chronicles of Tarrytown and Sleepy Hollow*, Edgar Mayhew Bacon talked about Irving's "delicious romance that he associated with the homestead when he made it the scene of the courtship. Mr. Irving was a frequent visitor to the old house, especially during the time his sister boarded there." He supposedly hinted to Elizabeth Mott that the party scene on that fateful night in "The Legend" was based on her house … and presumably the people there.

A mere jump in imagination could then position John Van Tassel as the model for plump old Baltus. As for his name, it didn't exist in Sleepy Hollow. Tarrytown newspaperman Daniel Van Tassel was John Van Tassel's great-grandson and did extensive research. "As to the names used by Irving, my knowledge of the records of the Old Dutch Church, as also of the county, manor and town records, enables me to say the name Baltus never was attached to any child in this vicinity," he concluded in an 1898 letter to the *New York Times*. "But examining the records of the old Albany County churches, I have come across it."

Ichabod Crane, Hapless Suitor

"The Legend" says: "Tall, but exceedingly lank, with narrow shoulders, long arms and legs, hands that dangled a mile out of his sleeves, feet that might have served as shovels, and his whole frame most loosely hung together. His head was small, and flat at top, with huge ears, large green glassy eyes, and a long snipe nose that looked like a weather-cock, perched upon his spindle neck, to tell which way the wind blew."

Storyteller and Babysitter. Ichabod liked to ingratiate himself with the farmers he boarded with, whose children he taught during the day.

Ichabod Crane's remains won't be found at the Old Dutch. After his encounter with the Headless Horseman in "The Legend," he disappeared: "The brook was searched but the body of the schoolmaster was not to be discovered." The mystery then intensifies. New intelligence comes after an old farmer visits New York and reports back to his Sleepy Hollow friends that Ichabod is still alive. Irving wrote, "He had left the neighborhood, partly through fear of the goblin and partly in mortification at having been suddenly dismissed by the heiress."

So what's true? At the Asbury Methodist Cemetery on Staten Island, there is a well-known name on a marble marker: Ichabod B. Crane. Irving knew Crane, according to local historians, when they met during the War of 1812. But while Ichabod B. Crane may have been the namesake, according to some tales he followed a similar career path in his later years to Revolutionary War hero Samuel Youngs. Like the imaginary Ichabod Crane, Youngs was a schoolteacher who studied law and became a state assemblyman. Youngs was buried at the Old Dutch in 1839. (His remains were transferred in 1851 to Ossining's new Dale Cemetery.)

But wait! In Andrew Burstein's 2007 book *The Original Knickerbocker: The Life of Washington Irving*, he proposes a different Ichabod. The model: schoolteacher Jesse Merwin of Kinderhook, N.Y.

While staying in Kinderhook in 1809, Irving wrote about a friendship with "a schoolmaster who teaches in the area—a pleasant good natured fellow." Who was it? "His new talkable companion, one year his junior," writes Burstein, "was Jesse Merwin whom Irving would later immortalize as 'Ichabod Crane.'" Burstein acknowledges, however, that Irving's literary executor and biographer, Pierre M.

> " THE CHIEF PART OF THESE STORIES, HOWEVER, TURNED UPON THE FAVORITE SPECTER OF SLEEPY HOLLOW, THE HEADLESS HORSEMAN, WHO HAD BEEN HEARD SEVERAL TIMES OF LATE, PATROLLING THE COUNTRY; AND, IT WAS SAID, TETHERED HIS HORSE NIGHTLY AMONG THE GRAVES IN THE CHURCHYARD."
>
> —WASHINGTON IRVING, "THE LEGEND OF SLEEPY HOLLOW," 1819–20

Brom Bones, Church Clerk

In 1797, when the Old Dutch congregation was a hundred years old, the consistory elected Abraham Van Tassel as clerk. He agreed to serve "gratis and without any donation." One duty was to read from his Bible (pictured above) every Sunday.

This Abraham was known as Brom Bones to set him apart from the other Abrahams in the village. It was the nickname Washington Irving used in his "Legend" for the practical joker who impersonated the Headless Horseman. Evidently, Brom Bones and several cronies were in Mr. William See's store when the first copy of "The Legend" reached Tarrytown. The ensuing excitement of what happened is captured by Edgar Mayhew Bacon in Chronicles of Tarrytown and Sleepy Hollow: *"No longer 'Brom, the devil,' but old uncle Abr'm Van Tassel, the patriarch listened in great wrath when someone told him that Washington Irving had put him in a book. Grasping his ponderous stick, he started for the door.*

"'Hole on, Uncle Brom! where you goin' so fast?' they cried.

"'Goin' to lick that writin' feller till he can't see!' roared the newly immortalized."

Irving, denied the Ichabod Crane–Jesse Merwin connection. Burstein concludes: "There is some question as to whether Merwin was really Irving's model for Ichabod, but there is little doubt that Merwin himself thought so. Suffice it to say that Merwin of Kinderhook appears to have given at least some inspiration."

Brom Bones, the Roystering Rival

> "The Legend" says: "A burly, roaring, roystering blade, the hero of the country round, which rang with his feats of strength and hardihood. From his Herculean frame, he had received the nickname of Brom Bones."

Who was Brom Bones? In "The Legend," the burly competitor for Katrina's heart was Abraham, or according to the preferred Dutch abbreviation, Brom Van Brunt, "foremost at all races and cockfights" and always ready for a "fight or a frolic." In fact, a "Brom Bones" actually worshipped at the Old Dutch and served with Captain Gabriel Requa's company in the Revolutionary War. Daniel Van Tassel, editor of the *Tarrytown Argus*, sent a letter to the *New York Times* in 1898 to help clear up the mystery of Brom's identity:

> *Before, during and after the Revolution there resided in Sleepy Hollow an Abraham Van Tassel, the younger brother of John Van Tassel, my great-grandfather. He was tall, spare, and large-boned. To distinguish him from others of the same name, he was called "Brom Bones." [On] an original Revolutionary muster roll of Capt. Gabriel Requa's company, this name appears upon the list, "Abraham Van Tassel (Bones)." There could be no mistaking the person meant.*

Abraham was of "gentle disposition, with a decidedly religious turn," said Daniel Van Tassel. "He quietly cultivated his fields, reared a large family, and regularly of a Sunday attended the services held at the Old Dutch Church of Sleepy Hollow, of which he was a member, and for some years its *voorleser* (leader in singing and reading). I believe that Irving got the nickname 'Brom Bones' from our locality, but it is possible that the original Brom Van Brunt was of Kinderhook."

The Kinderhook Controversy

Where Did "The Legend" Take Place?

An old tourist brochure from Kinderhook, N.Y., a picturesque village in the Hudson Valley a hundred miles north of Sleepy Hollow, says about the Van Alen House:

Local tradition has it that Washington Irving, who was a tutor in nearby Lindenwald [residence of Judge Van Ness], used this dwelling for the scene of the famous party at the home of Katrina Van Tassel in his story "The Legend of Sleepy Hollow.

What? Not Sleepy Hollow? Is this true? The basis for the Kinderhook claim is Irving's two-month visit to the village after the death in 1809 of his fiancée, Matilda Hoffman.

There's more ... In the late nineteenth century, a debate played out in the letters column of the *New York Times*. Author Harold Van Santvoord of Kinderhook fired an early shot in his letter published February 26, 1898:

At this time [Irving] formed a close intimacy with [schoolmaster] Jesse Merwin, the Ichabod Crane of the comic portrait in the "Sketch Book," who was also staying at Lindenwald ... Winter evenings [were spent] cracking jokes and spinning yarns with Katrina Van Tassel and Brom Bones in the quaint old Dutch kitchen of a neighboring farmhouse.

He continued, "Many believe it was Irving's original intention to locate the scene of the legend in Kinderhook."

Tempers flared in written responses. In one, Tarrytown writer Edgar Mayhew Bacon replied tersely: "Mr. Van Santvoord has made up his mind that Irving's 'Legend of Sleepy Hollow' would look well at Kinderhook. Whether this is an attempt to foster a boom at Kinderhook or merely the amusement of an idle hour are not questions which can be discussed."

After a letter from Daniel Van Tassel, published May 28, 1898, the debate quieted. A newspaperman from Tarrytown and a descendant of Revolutionary soldier John Van Tassel, the writer offered this conclusion on "The Legend's" location:

I strongly agree the geography of the legend belongs to Tarrytown. The description of Sleepy

Hollow is correct; the picture of the Old Dutch Church and its surrounding territory is remarkably true to nature. No one can mistake the author's plain intention.

In piecing together the rest of the legend, Daniel Van Tassel concedes that the model for Ichabod did come from a teacher in Kinderhook, Jesse Merwin. But he was puzzled about a log schoolhouse, which never existed in Sleepy Hollow. "The pre-Revolutionary schoolhouses of this neighborhood are well known," he said. "There never was a log schoolhouse. Mr. Van Santvoord says that the schoolhouse that Merwin taught in at Kinderhook was built of logs. This answers my oft-repeated query. Irving in his poetic fancy transferred it and its teacher to Sleepy Hollow. We admit his right and gratefully accept his story."

Did Irving Visit Here? Kinderhook's Van Alen House is open for tours.

Washington in New York. Irving was 26, living in New York, when this 1809 portrait was made by John Wesley Jarvis.
Photo: Historic Hudson Valley.

SLEEPY HOLLOW COUNTRY

Jim Logan of Sleepy Hollow Cemetery has written about places of interest in "Sleepy Hollow Country," as Washington Irving called the area around the Old Dutch Church. Who can forget the terrifying encounter of the Headless Horseman and Ichabod Crane at the Pocantico Bridge? Or Ichabod's first glimpse of the Horseman at the fateful site of Major André's capture? Trace Ichabod's famous ride up the old Albany Post Road (now called Broadway) and explore other places of interest around Tarrytown.

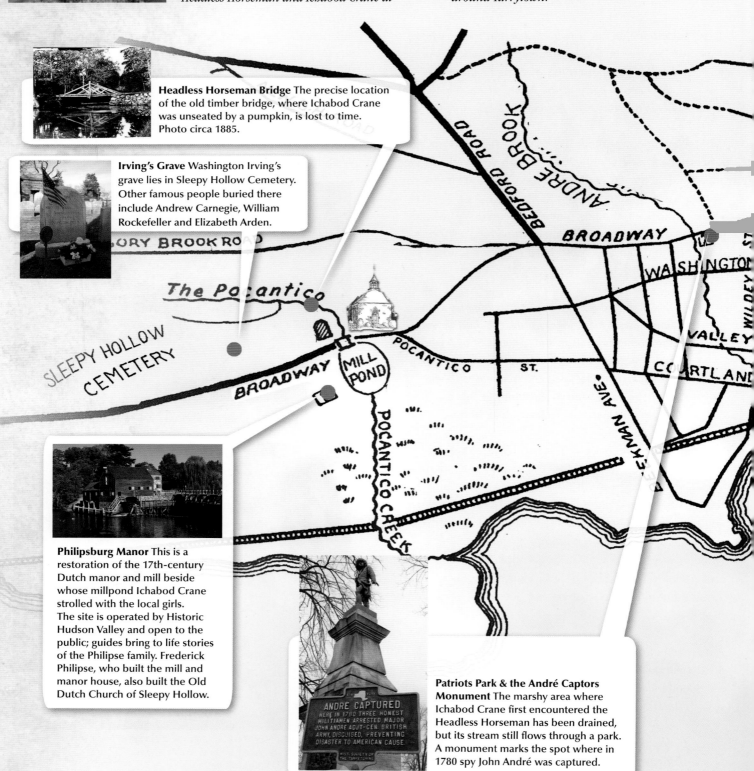

Headless Horseman Bridge The precise location of the old timber bridge, where Ichabod Crane was unseated by a pumpkin, is lost to time. Photo circa 1885.

Irving's Grave Washington Irving's grave lies in Sleepy Hollow Cemetery. Other famous people buried there include Andrew Carnegie, William Rockefeller and Elizabeth Arden.

Philipsburg Manor This is a restoration of the 17th-century Dutch manor and mill beside whose millpond Ichabod Crane strolled with the local girls. The site is operated by Historic Hudson Valley and open to the public; guides bring to life stories of the Philipse family. Frederick Philipse, who built the mill and manor house, also built the Old Dutch Church of Sleepy Hollow.

Patriots Park & the André Captors Monument The marshy area where Ichabod Crane first encountered the Headless Horseman has been drained, but its stream still flows through a park. A monument marks the spot where in 1780 spy John André was captured.

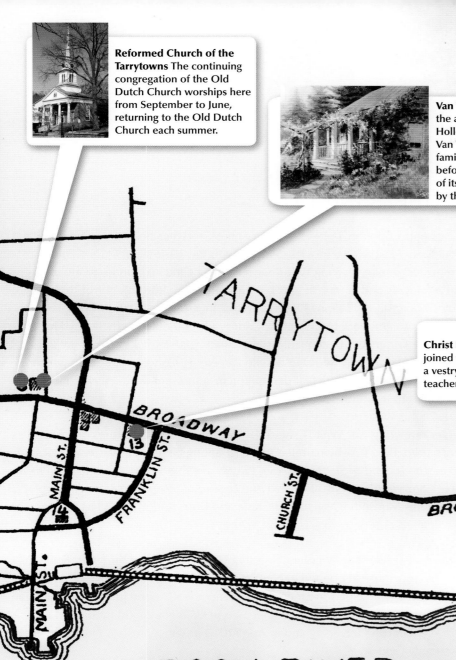

Reformed Church of the Tarrytowns The continuing congregation of the Old Dutch Church worships here from September to June, returning to the Old Dutch Church each summer.

Van Tassel/Mott House Van Tassels had long populated the area when Irving wrote "The Legend of Sleepy Hollow." Historian Edgar Mayhew Bacon attaches Katrina Van Tassel's party to a stone house built by the Martling family in the early 1700s. It became the Van Tassel Tavern before the Revolution, and was later known by the name of its new owner, Jacob Mott. The site is occupied today by the Landmark Condominium.

Christ Episcopal Church Irving joined the church in 1848 and was a vestryman, warden, Sunday school teacher and regular parishioner.

HUDSON RIVER

Sunnyside Washington Irving's meticulously restored home is filled with the writer's possessions, including his writing desk. Sunnyside is now the property of Historic Hudson Valley and open for tours.

> "'RIP VAN WINKLE' AND THE 'LEGEND OF SLEEPY HOLLOW' RANK AMONG THE MOST DELIGHTFUL AND POPULAR TALES EVER WRITTEN. IN OUR COUNTRY THEY HAVE BEEN READ, I BELIEVE, BY NEARLY EVERYBODY WHO CAN READ AT ALL."
>
> —WILLIAM CULLEN BRYANT

"THE LEGEND" LIVES ON

Since its publication in 1819–20, Irving's ghost story has been the spine-tingling subject for at least twelve movies. Starting with the 1922 silent classic *The Headless Horseman,* starring Will Rogers, "The Legend" continues to attract big-name producers and actors. In 1999, for instance, Tim Burton's horror thriller *Sleepy Hollow* starred Johnny Depp as police investigator Ichabod Crane, who was sent from New York to look into a series of brutal murders in Sleepy Hollow, which were committed by a headless horseman (Christopher Walken). In 2013 a supernatural drama TV series also called *Sleepy Hollow* premiered, in which Ichabod Crane sets out to defeat demon forces in present-day Sleepy Hollow. By 2017, it was in its fourth season.

A lighter rendering was Walt Disney's 1949 classic, *The Adventures of Ichabod and Mr. Toad.* Bing Crosby narrated this enchanting cartoon. It was re-released in 1958 as *The Legend of Sleepy Hollow.* On March 5, 1958, an episode of *Shirley Temple's Storybook* on NBC featured *The Legend of Sleepy Hollow.* Temple played Katrina, Jules Munshin was Ichabod Crane and Boris Karloff served as the stand-in storyteller.

Broadway also saw spooky potential in Irving's "Legend." But, in 1948, when the *Sleepy Hollow* musical opened in New York, with George Lessner's lively tunes, it lasted for only twelve performances. An operatic debut came in 2009 at Michigan State University. That same year another *Sleepy Hollow* musical premiered at Utah's Weber State University and in April 2010 it won a musical theater award at the Kennedy Center.

Over the years "The Legend" has been reprinted countless times. Schools and towns from Irving, Texas, to Irvington, New York, found inspiration in using the author's name, as did companies such as the Irving Trust Company, which later merged with the Bank of New York. Even the U.S. Postal Service issued commemorative stamps: Washington Irving (1940) and "The Legend of Sleepy Hollow" (1974). Bicentennial celebrations of the author's birth occurred in 1983 at the New-York Historical Society, Columbia University, and overseas in Spain, where Irving served as minister.

Now, nearly 200 years since its date of publication, the unforgettable "Legend of Sleepy Hollow" continues to attract national and international visitors to the Old Dutch Church and Burying Ground. Tens of thousands of people flock to the area, especially around Halloween, for the chilling "Legend" reenactments at the church, the Old Dutch Church Fest, as well as the Historic Hudson Valley's Scary Horseman Hollow and Great Jack O'Lantern Blaze.

Scared Yet? "The Legend" continues its bone-chilling attraction, from movies—Will Rogers in 1922's *Headless Horseman* (top) and Johnny Depp in 1999's *Sleepy Hollow*—to stamps; the U.S. Postal Service issued a 1940 portrait of Irving and a 1974 commemorative stamp of Sleepy Hollow. *Sleepy Hollow* movie poster: Paramount Pictures.

CHAPTER 7

LIFE IN THE HOLLOW,
1800s

As the old century with its memories of war and hardship faded away, the Old Dutch Church finally enjoyed a period of stability and growth. From never having had a permanent pastor before the Revolution, the church was never without one afterward. Several were larger than life, truly remarkable men. But fire, decay and a church bursting at the seams—literally—soon spoiled the tranquility of Sleepy Hollow, and the congregation built two impressive new churches to the south in Tarrytown. What happened to the beloved church in the Hollow?

A Different Look. This 1861 painting by W. R. Miller shows the neoclassical portico, built in 1837, on the new entrance. Twenty years later, after the portico decayed, it was replaced with a small stone platform and steps. Illustration: Historic Hudson Valley. Previous page: Currier & Ives, 1867.

MINISTERS, AT LAST

As soon as the American Revolutionary War passed into history, the congregation turned its attention to the responsibilities of ownership. They tossed out the old cushioned and canopied "thrones"—there would be no more special privileges for the Philipses—and installed box seating for the elders and deacons. The uncomfortable oak benches were replaced with straight-backed pine pews. (The next generation would find these only slightly less uncomfortable and tear them out in 1837.) The church registered its charter with the Westchester County Clerk in 1786 and, most important, hired its first full-time pastor.

He Dared to Use English!

The congregation of the newly renamed Reformed Dutch Church on Philipse Manor chose **Rev. Stephen Van Voorhees** of Rhinebeck, N.Y., as their pastor. Long a proponent of separation from the Reformed Church in Holland, he was the first to be licensed by the independent American Reformed Church in 1772.

Rev. Van Voorhees had his work cut out for him. For ten years there had been no regular visits from clergy. As the new minister, on Sunday, September 25, 1785, he would celebrate his first sacrament of baptism. After his sermon and a prayer, Rev. Van Voorhees descended from the pedestal pulpit. Glancing over the congregation, now more nearly at eye level, he made the customary presentation and invited those parents who had children to be baptized to step forward.

First to present their child was Solomon Hawes and his wife, Levina Hammond, a relative of the famous militia commander Col. James Hammond, who was present as a witness. As the clergyman took the infant out of her father's arms and pronounced, "Levine, I baptize thee," looks of astonishment crossed members' faces. He was baptizing little Levine Hawes ... in *English!*

It wasn't that they didn't understand the language; English was in common use outside the church. But inside these stone walls, Dutch was traditional. As historian Edgar Mayhew Bacon wrote, "Revolutions would do well enough in State, but in Church they would have none of them."

" THE BELL CRIES TRIUMPHANTLY IN EVERY BELIEVER: 'IF AS OUR JUDGE GOD IS SATISFIED; IF AS OUR FATHER HE LOVES US; IF AS THE CONTROLLER OF ALL EVENTS HE WILL MAKE ALL THINGS TO WORK TOGETHER FOR OUR GOOD; IF ALL HE IS AND HAS AND DOES IS FOR US, HIS PEOPLE—WHO CAN BE AGAINST US? WHO OF ALL THE CONQUERED ENEMIES OF THE CROSS CAN SAFELY BE AGAINST US IN OUR PROGRESS TOWARD HEAVEN?"

—REV. ABEL T. STEWART, PASTOR, OLD DUTCH CHURCH, 1866

History in the Making. Top: The church's 1786 charter was recorded in the County Clerk's Office in White Plains, N.Y. The church became known at that time as the Reformed Dutch Church on Philipse Manor. The original single-page handwritten charter has deteriorated. Middle: After the Revolution, the church started a new English baptism register. Bottom: The first entry was Levine Hawes's baptism, which caused a furor.

Levine was the only child baptized that day. Perhaps other parents froze in their tracks, wondering if a child baptized in English was really baptized at all. But on the next Sunday a few progressive parents stepped forward, and for the next few Sundays came a parade of parents with children of all ages, until pent-up demand was satisfied. In two months, Rev. Van Voorhees baptized sixty-seven children! And he kept the church registers in English, a new tradition continued ever after.

But some members of the congregation did not quickly forgive the minister's offense. After three years, Rev. Van Voorhees found a new position elsewhere.

"Interminable Sermons"

Their next pastor, **John Frelinghuysen Jackson**, was a wealthy, cultured gentleman of Scottish and Dutch heritage. A tall, fine-looking man, Rev. Jackson arrived in 1791 fresh from the seminary. Several of his ancestors were distinguished for their character and eloquence in the pulpit, and Jackson was held in high repute by his ministerial brethren.

His congregation at the Old Dutch Church, however, thought him proud. He *powdered* his hair and was always *patting* it, and never spoke to any of his flock whom he met on the road. When he rode up from Harlem on horseback on Saturday, stopping overnight at a congregant's home, he'd *order* his horse be put up. When he wanted the horse again, he'd *order* it to be saddled.

Was it Rev. Jackson who Washington Irving had in mind when he wrote about the "interminable sermons" he'd heard at the church as a teen while visiting Tarrytown in 1798? (See Irving quote, facing page.)

REV. JOHN FRELINGHUYSEN JACKSON.
Pastor from 1791 to 1806.

After fifteen years Rev. Jackson left the little Dutch church over some trouble that grew out of a consistory member's "too free use of his tongue," as one of his successors wrote. As part of the last worship service he conducted there, Rev. Jackson read Isaac Watts's Psalm 120, rephrased as a hymn. When he came to the fifth verse, he turned and glared down at the man who'd caused the trouble, while loudly intoning:

New passions still their souls engage,
And keep their malice strong:
What shall be done to curb thy rage,
O thou devouring tongue!

His departure in 1806 paved the way for a successor two years later, whom the congregation would find very much to their liking.

Eloquent, but "Covered in Snuff"

By all accounts, **Rev. Thomas Gibson Smith** was a large man made larger than life by the extraordinary impact he had on people. Genial and kindly and social in nature, it was said he was careless in his personal habits to the point that he was sometimes "covered in snuff from head to foot." But when he preached, his eloquence thrilled listeners. A Scotsman, he had immigrated to New York shortly before the Revolution and enlisted in the Continental army, where he served as a lieutenant. Afterward, he taught school for a while, then studied for the ministry and was licensed by the Associated Presbyterian Church.

His preaching was full of feeling, powerful in denunciation of sin and strong in appeal to the sinner. Moreover, his ministry was marked by revivals, so interest in religion ran high and many new people joined the church. During these "times of refreshing," word traveled up and down the Hudson River, and captains of the river sloops would come ashore with their men to enjoy the evening weekday service and receive a blessing. On Wednesday, January 15, 1817, at one of these revival meetings, eighty-nine people were added to the membership register! But then comes a lengthy gap in church records; perhaps record-keeping grew onerous during this exciting time, or records were simply lost. The member register doesn't resume until after Rev. Smith's retirement twenty years later.

Rev. Smith had a Scotsman's sense of humor. One Sunday morning he was vexed to find person after person asleep during his sermon. "Fire! Fire!" he shouted.

"Where's the fire?" they cried, struggling to their feet.

"Where's the fire?" he thundered down at them. "In hell—for such sleepy Christians as you are!"

Like preachers of the previous century, Rev. Smith had an extended parish. He supervised the Presbyterian meeting house in Elmsford, organized the Reformed Church in Hawthorne and preached to large audiences in the White Plains Courthouse until a new Presbyterian church was built.

At times, his wife was no admirer of the good reverend. Rev. Smith had married Jemima Allen while he was teaching, and she had helped him study for the ministry. The couple had seven daughters, two of whom died when they were

"SCARCELY HAD THE PREACHER HELD FORTH FOR HALF AN HOUR, ON ONE OF HIS INTERMINABLE SERMONS, THAN IT SEEMED AS IF THE DROWSY INFLUENCE OF SLEEPY HOLLOW BREATHED INTO THE PLACE: ONE BY ONE THE CONGREGATION SANK INTO SLUMBER; THE SANCTIFIED ELDERS LEANED BACK IN THEIR PEWS, SPREADING THEIR HANDKERCHIEFS OVER THEIR FACES, AS IF TO KEEP OFF FLIES; WHILE THE LOCUSTS IN THE TREES WOULD SPIN OUT THEIR SULTRY SUMMER NOTES, AS IF IN IMITATION OF THE SLEEP-PROVOKING TONES OF THE DOMINIE."

—WASHINGTON IRVING,
"SLEEPY HOLLOW,"
KNICKERBOCKER, 1839

Thomas Smith. His grave is by the wall of the church he loved.

A Curious Resolution

This resolution by the consistory was recorded in the church minutes on December 6, 1809, and honors a prominent family in the community:

"The consistory, recognizing the ancient right of the family of the Philipse and Van Cortlandt, resolved that a seat should be erected in the church of Philipsburg for the use and benefit of said family, whose local situation will admit their attending the worship of God in said church, and that the Rev. Thomas G. Smith and Thos. Boyce, Elder, be a committee to wait upon the family of Mr. Beekman to receive their approbation of the above resolution and report to the Consistory."

Gerard G. Beekman Jr. had purchased Upper Mills after the Revolution, and he and his wife Cornelia Van Cortlandt Beekman, an ardent Patriot during the Revolution, lived in the manor house. Cornelia's great-aunt was Lady Catherine Philipse, whose husband Lord Frederick Philipse built the church.

teenagers. Though Jemima was said to have had a masterful mind, by the end of her life she was seen as erratic and manifestly unbalanced. Exasperated by her husband's carelessness—often, tobacco juice stained Rev. Smith's whiskers and evidence of his last meal was on his shirt—Jemima once locked him in his study before the service.

On another day she rode his horse up and down in front of the church, making so much noise the congregation couldn't hear the sermon. Jemima had a good command of the Scriptures and, from her chair by the stove, which stood in front of the pulpit, she would correct her husband while he was preaching. Sometimes, she even stretched out on a front pew and snored through the sermon.

After the consistory suspended her from Communion, Jemima held a grudge against the man who read the announcement in church. He came to her house one day to ask the pastor to attend a funeral. Rev. Smith was away. When Jemima refused to take a message, the man asked to wait. She locked him in a room for four hours!

Rev. Smith bore her behavior calmly and treated her kindly. When she died, he buried her next to their two daughters in the churchyard. In all, he served the congregation for twenty-nine years, retiring shortly before he died in April 1837, age eighty-two. He was buried next to his wife and two daughters in the churchyard.

Mourning the loss of a warrior for the faith, the Classis, which supervised New York Reformed churches, issued this statement: "No new theology with its fine-spun theories dimmed his clear vision; no lack of faith weakened his arm. His voice gave forth no uncertain sound. Like a true Christian knight he kept his armor bright, and for a target held firm his red-cross shield, until at last they laid him down to sleep near by the walls of the dear Old Church he loved so well."

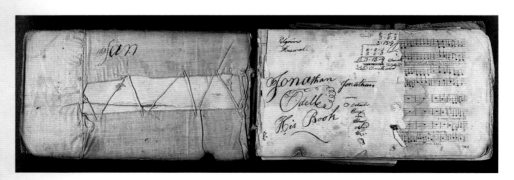

"His Book." Well-worn hymnbook belonging to Jonathan Odell (d. 1818, age 87), war hero, tavern owner and church trustee. Note the handmade cloth cover and "His Book" under the signature.

Historic Tavern. Rev. Thomas Smith drew crowds wherever he preached, including this tavern owned by Jonathan Odell, "the father of all the Odells," as Smith called him. The house, built before 1700 by elder Jan Harmse, still stands in Irvington, just south of Dows Lane on Broadway.
Illustration: Westchester County Historical Society.

FIRE AT THE CHURCH!

Nearly 300 people joined the church between 1785 and 1817, the year the membership register ends during Rev. Smith's ministry. The pine pews were surely crowded at Sunday worship services. No question, Tarrytown was growing. Since 1835 the famed writer Washington Irving had made Sunnyside in Tarrytown his permanent home. New York City merchants and men of wealth and refinement began moving up to the village. The beauty of the location and its easy access to the city by stagecoach and steamboat attracted many. But to some, the Old Dutch Church in Sleepy Hollow, as Irving had translated the old Dutch name of Slaepershaven, seemed too countrified.

Heating in winter was unsatisfactory, to say the least. Pipes ran from a stove in front of the pulpit through a glass windowpane. The smoke was dreadful, painful to eyes and lungs. As one pastor wrote, it "could not have been endured by congregations less devout than were those of the good days of old." To combat the cold, farmers came to church with footstoves and bricks, which they heated before the service began—and reheated during the service, if necessary.

The church needed major repairs. On June 30, 1835, this consensus was recorded in the minutes: "Whereas the House belonging to the Congregation of the Dutch church at or near Tarrytown is no longer fit to worship in, being rather in a dangerous state by some part of the wall giving way and moreover from the

A Special Gift. In 1836, Domine Thomas Smith presented this Bible to Steuben Swartwout, a member of the congregation.

101

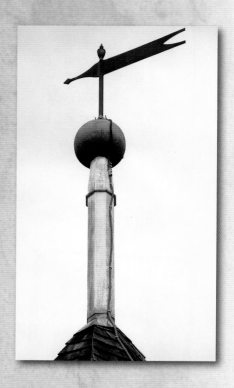

"Let Him Dunder!"

Despite the fire in 1837 that damaged the belfry and roof, the church did not have protection against lightning strikes until the 1990s. An 1840 item in Knickerbocker *magazine gives a tongue-in-cheek report—perhaps written by Irving himself—about a church member who refused to vote for a proposal to install a lightning rod: "We've been to great deal droubles, and great deal 'spence, to build a house for God Almitis; and now if he's a mind to dunder on his own house, and burn him up, let him dunder den! I shan't vote for de dunder rod!"*

increase in the number of the inhabitants of the village of Tarrytown, we think that the time is come that divine Providence points out to us that there ought to be a church built in the village."

A church in the village center in Tarrytown wasn't a new idea. Fifteen years earlier, on December 20, 1820, a resolution had been proposed and accepted that "there be preaching in the lower neighborhood." Although $900 in pledges was collected for a new church, including $50 from Rev. Smith (a fifth of his annual salary), the effort did not immediately succeed.

Instead, another collection was taken for the repair of the Old Dutch Church, and $475 was donated by church families, including the Stormses, Dutchers, Sees, Martlings, Pauldings, Yerkses, Van Warts, Beekmans, Van Tassels, Boyces, Devoes, Minnerlys, Orsers, Foshays, Jewels and Hunts. Presumably, repairs made the church at least "fit for worship."

In August 1837, the members called **Rev. George DuBois** (pictured below) to be their minister. Of Huguenot descent, he was born in New Paltz about 1800 and had spent nineteen years at the Franklin Street Church in New York City. He accepted under the condition that a new church be built in Tarrytown.

This time the effort succeeded. Abraham and Julia Storms donated a building lot in the heart of the village, a mile south of the old church. To raise money, a committee began soliciting pledges. The church sold land. Members loaned the church money, as did the Collegiate Church in New York. In late 1837 construction began, and the Greek Revival–style building at 42 North Broadway was completed the next year.

The new building, dubbed South Church, was grand—brick, fronted by four Ionic columns and surmounted with a steeple. The inscription on the stone high over the porch bears the words addressed to Moses after he received the Ten Commandments and is from Exodus 20:24: "In all places where I record my name, I will come unto thee, and I will bless thee."

Almost as if it felt a sense of neglect, the Old Dutch Church, already in a deteriorated state, suffered another major blow: a fire. In a pouring rainstorm in 1837, a streak of lightning struck the belfry and ran like liquid fire down the

Height of Modernity. In 1837, this new pulpit replaced the seventeenth-century Dutch pedestal pulpit. It, in turn, was replaced in the late 1890s with a replica of the original pulpit.
Photo: Westchester County Historical Society.

Myth or Fact

Remnants of the Original Pulpit?

Was this book cabinet made from pieces of the seventeenth-century pulpit? According to tradition, the old pulpit was sold and pieces of it were made into a secretary for the pastor's office. Rev. Gerald Vander Hart recalls this tall cabinet from his office at First Reformed Church when he started as its minister in 1972. "The first pulpit may have been a simpler design," he says. "If so, the plain pilasters on the top of the secretary could possibly have come from the original pulpit."

old timbers, which burst into flames. Afterward, church members discovered the smoking belfry and damaged roof. To their credit, the congregation chose not to abandon the old church. Many felt a strong attachment to it, while others who lived nearby preferred it over the more distant new church. So the elders and deacons began a vigorous campaign to raise money for repairs. As Clarence E. Bacon, clerk of consistory at First Reformed, wrote a hundred years later:

> *When we consider that the new church (and parsonage) cost between six and seven thousand dollars, and the repairs to the old church cost over two thousand dollars, we wonder at the courage of the people. And our wonder grows when we recall that the year 1837 witnessed the worst financial panic that this country had ever seen. It waited until 1929 to see anything as bad as that and the depression that followed.*

Indeed, the "repairs" of 1837 gave quite a bold new look to the Old Dutch Church! The congregation took the opportunity to make a few structural changes, starting with a new door in the west wall that faced the Albany Post Road, newly rerouted because of the Croton Aqueduct project. A one-story Greek Revival portico dressed up the entrance. Other repairs may have altered the roofline, since this type of roof was not known in this area before about 1720, long after the church was erected. Also, a stovepipe was extended through the roof. Windows were enlarged and given a Gothic arch, and the old door became a window.

Inside, workers hid the barrel ceiling with a flat false ceiling, perhaps to help in

heating the church. The whitewashed stone walls were plastered over, the shallow north gallery removed and the west gallery enlarged. New, wider pews with angled backs conceded slightly more comfort for the congregation. As for the old narrow, straight-backed pine pews installed after the Revolution, they were moved upstairs to the expanded gallery.

Uncomfortable for Over 300 Years. These pews, installed in the church post-Revolution, were replaced and moved to the gallery in 1837. The flame-grain, quarter-sawn oak seats in some of these pews may date from the original church construction.

Regrettably, the consistory had the pedestal pulpit torn out and replaced with a low, modern pulpit. Why it was removed—whether due to damage or decay or changing tastes—we have no record. Nor do we know what happened to it. One tradition says the original pulpit was put in storage with the stairs and sounding board and later sold and that pieces of it were used in making a bookcase. In any case, in 1866, Rev. Abel T. Stewart wrote that "scarcely a vestige of it can be found."

By some accounts, the seventeenth-century Dutch Communion table was sold to a local judge for $25, and later reclaimed by Washington Irving's good friend, James Paulding. According to a church history written by Rev. Stewart in 1866, "When the workmen had finished, the church had need of their ancient article of furniture. James Paulding generously purchased it at the price paid for it by Judge Constant, restored it to its original beauty at an additional expense of $15, and returned it to the church, where it has ever since been held in higher and more general appreciation."

AN AMICABLE PARTING

By 1838, Rev. DuBois found himself pastor of a congregation that worshipped in two buildings. He preached at the Old Dutch Church on Sunday mornings and at the South Church in the afternoons. He was described by Rev. David Cole as a "lovingly genial" man whose dignity "sat on him like a gracefully fitting garment." He was said to give "deeply spiritual and nourishing" sermons. For the double duty, the consistory paid him $700 a year, more than twice Rev. Smith's salary.

To finance the upkeep of two churches, the consistory came up with a plan to rent the pews, starting November 24, 1838. The pew rents were an important source of funds. In 1850, for example, pew rentals and donations collected for both churches totaled $906. Pew rents continued until 1888, when the present envelope and pledge system was adopted.

The practice of preaching in both churches was continued by **Rev. Joseph Wilson** when he arrived from Fairfield, N.J., in 1844. But a division was growing, between those who did not want to leave the old church and those who lived in the village of Tarrytown and preferred a more accessible place of worship.

By mid-century Tarrytown was a flourishing country community of almost 2,000 people, with a railroad, a busy port and a lively farmers' market. Washington Irving continued to be a vital part of the community until his death in 1859. The Dutch Reformed church was still the religious home of most of the community, although other churches had sprung up, including Episcopal (attended by Irving), Methodist and Catholic churches.

Rev. John Mason Ferris (pictured below), son of an eminent minister and New York University chancellor, became the minister in the fall of 1849. He was young and "full of good judgment and energy," according to Rev. David Cole, who knew him. He quickly realized the attendance was much larger in the South Church and when cold weather arrived, he declined to preach in the old church building.

To solve the dilemma, the consistory engaged an assistant minister, **Rev. John W. Schenck,** to perform pastoral duties for the members who attended services in the old church, but he resigned after a few months. The 164-year-old building's future hung in precarious balance ...

In September 1851, church elders and deacons met to consider once again how

best to obtain a minister to hold services at the Old Dutch Church. On November 8, they decided the best course of action would be to formally divide the congregation into two separate churches.

What happened next? At two-thirty on Monday afternoon, November 24, 1851, about a hundred people gathered in the South Church in Tarrytown to organize a new, separate church. With heavy snowstorms upstate, it was probably overcast and snowing in Tarrytown. Men, women and children, dressed in their "Sunday best" for the momentous occasion, arrived in carriages, wagons, on horseback and afoot. The street was still unpaved at this time, and in the snows of winter it was a slippery, muddy mess.

Crime and Punishment

Jealousy, swearing, drinking, quarreling, playing cards, missing church services for no good reason—in the nineteenth century any of these acts could get a member called up before the elders and deacons of the consistory.

1809 *A man complained that his wife "was impossible to live with." She confessed to improper language and promised to mend her ways.*

1810 *A man refused to admit that he had "in an unwarranted manner" tried to correct a slave. Membership privileges were suspended.*

1817 *A wife confessed to scratching her husband's face because she suspected him of "criminal conduct with another woman," and promised "never more."*

1822 *A member was accused of "keeping a disorderly house, viz. suffering card-playing therein."*

1842 *A woman acknowledged the birth of her second illegitimate child. The consistory suspended her from membership privileges.*

1845 *When a church member left for the Baptist church, the consistory resolved "that her name be erased from the records."*

1848 *Witnesses testifying on behalf of a woman accused of running a "house of ill fame" asserted that nothing improper happened. She was acquitted.*

South Church (aka Second Reformed). The grandest building in the village when it was built in 1837–38, the "clock-tower church" in Tarrytown is shown with its original steeple, replaced in the late 1870s after it was struck by lightning and burned.

Rev. Philip Phelps of Hastings conducted devotionals. Rev. John L. See of Unionville preached a sermon titled, "A Joy of Many Generations," from Isaiah 60:15. After the services seventy-five persons presented their letters of membership to the newly organized Second Reformed Church.

The new members included Abraham and Julia Storms, who had donated the land for the church and parsonage. Other families included the Sees, Van Winkles, Archers, Martlings, Vanderbilts, Vails and Wildeys. Later, in their nightly devotions, they undoubtedly prayed that they had done the right thing. Indeed, that church would prosper.

Now more uncertainty faced the Old Dutch Church ... In exchange for $2,000 cash and relief from a debt of about $1,000, Old Dutch's congregation gave up claim to all church property in the village of Tarrytown, including the nearly new church building and parsonage. Could the old church survive?

RESCUED BY A REVEREND

No minister. A small building unsuited for expansion. No parsonage. Not enough money to build one ... Of 150 members remaining on the membership roll of the Old Dutch Church, "full 40 were either such as could not be found, or such as we have sought for good reasons to be relieved of," as the next minister, **Rev. Abel T. Stewart,** would later describe the situation he faced when he became pastor.

The new pastor struggled deeply with the best course of action. "For the disproportionate character of this division, I have never been able to account," a puzzled Rev. Stewart wrote in his "Historical Discourse," an address he delivered to the congregation in 1866. "It would seem not to have occurred to your minds that if you attempted to confine yourselves to your old church edifice you must utterly die out and that if you left it, it would be worse than nothing to you in value, nor that the money you have received was not more than half enough to obtain for you even a parsonage."

First Church. The Old Dutch Church erected this building in North Tarrytown (now Sleepy Hollow) and moved into it in 1854, taking the name First Reformed. The top of the steeple decayed and was removed in the 1940s.

Still, this congregation built a parsonage and within months was actually looking into building a new church. The congregation of the Old Dutch Church, which officially took the name of First Reformed Protestant Dutch Church of Tarrytown, or just "First Church," chose a site not far away, on Broadway near Beekman Avenue, in the northern end of Tarrytown.

Land was purchased for $1,250 and once again the congregation took out loans and built a Gothic-style church. (It would take ten years, until 1864, during the Civil War, for Rev. Stewart to repay the outstanding debt of $7,762. His account book lists contributors and donations ranging from two dollars to $650, including $10 from Washington Irving.) And in May 1854, First Church threw wide open its new doors!

From that time on the formula was simple: Winter and spring services in the well-heated new church, and summer and fall in the old church. It was a good compromise, meant to please everyone, but the attachment to the old church was still very strong. Even years after the new church was built, it was said that elder William Landrine continued to drive over every Sunday to the Old Dutch Church. After hitching his team of horses nearby, he would sit on the stone step in front of the old church, all alone, perhaps chilled to the bone, with his head resting upon his hand in silent and reverent meditation until the hour of worship had passed.

Pocantico Mission

By tradition, Sunday school groups met in the old church gallery. In the summer of 1867, Rev. John Bodine Thompson and the consistory established the Pocantico Mission, a Sunday school to serve the many poor immigrant children who lived near the Old Dutch Church. At the same time, he announced a "Visitor's Church" in July and August, with guest ministers preaching at morning and afternoon services. The children flocked to the school all summer, one group for those with some Christian education, and another for smaller children who lacked religious instruction of any kind. The younger children met under the trees in the churchyard.

By such faithfulness and love over the generations, with stewardship from church members, pastors and regular townspeople, the Old Dutch Church made it through its formative years after the American Revolution, made it through a fire, made it through what could have turned into a nasty local church schism, made it through the Civil War, and was ready to embrace the new twentieth century … a blessing to the community.

The Remarkable Reverend

One daring incident involving Rev. Stewart (pictured at left) stands out above all others. It had to do with the Civil War draft riots that swept through New York in 1863. The war was not popular with everyone in the North. Some were against forcing the Southern states to return to the Union. President Lincoln's policies were frequently opposed; partisanship was at fever pitch, also among church members. A persistent legend claims that Sleepy Hollow was an important stop for escaped slaves traveling a secretive route to Canada, known as the Underground Railroad. There is no evidence, but the spring house for the manor was said to be a safe house on the route.

Among workingmen, anger over compulsory military service led to riots near offices where the draft lists were kept, and to attacks on blacks, who were blamed for the war. Such lists were kept in Tarrytown, and at one point a confrontation loomed between the draft resisters and the government. In Chronicles of Tarrytown and Sleepy Hollow, *published 1897, church historian Edgar Mayhew Bacon gives an eyewitness account:*

> A band of several hundred rioters was reported to be on the road to Tarrytown. There was consternation in every home. Word came from unquestioned sources that the torch was to be applied to Tarrytown, and men armed themselves and secured the defenses to their houses as well as they were able to do. Over the hills a long line of Negroes fled to the woods to escape a threatened massacre.

> The rioters were within a short distance of the town, and no man in the community dared put himself in their way till Abel T. Stewart, minister of God's Word, accompanied by Captain Oscar Jones, a soldier home on furlough, marched out with splendid audacity to meet them ...

> Mr. Stewart met the rioters and reasoned with them. He told them that their reception would be warm; that a gunboat, which had just arrived in the river, would shell the houses of their sympathizers without mercy if they persisted; he used cogent reasoning, convincing even to such a bloodthirsty mob of anarchists; and in the end he succeeded in turning them back.

"THIS REBELLION IS MAKING WAR NOT ONLY AGAINST THE GOVERNMENT, BUT AGAINST GOD. FIGHTING FOR THE RIGHT TO KEEP MEN IN IGNORANCE OF GOD'S WILL, TO SEPARATE HUSBANDS AND WIVES, AND TO SNATCH AWAY THE INNOCENT AND HELPLESS OFFSPRING … CAN GOD BESTOW HIS BENEDICTION UPON AN ENTERPRISE LIKE THIS? NO, IT CANNOT BE."
—REV. ABEL STEWART, 1863

CHAPTER 8

KEEPING THE FAITH,
1897 TO TODAY

A changing world swirled around "the church on the knoll" without ever seeming to touch it. Sunbeams still slept quietly in the grass-covered yard. The old nineteenth century closed with a bicentennial celebration, keynoted by the soon-to-be U.S. President Theodore Roosevelt. Surprisingly, the congregation came full circle by reuniting two Dutch church congregations, and there was another gala celebration, this time for the church's 325th. And the bell? Could its fabulous story still be ringing out today?

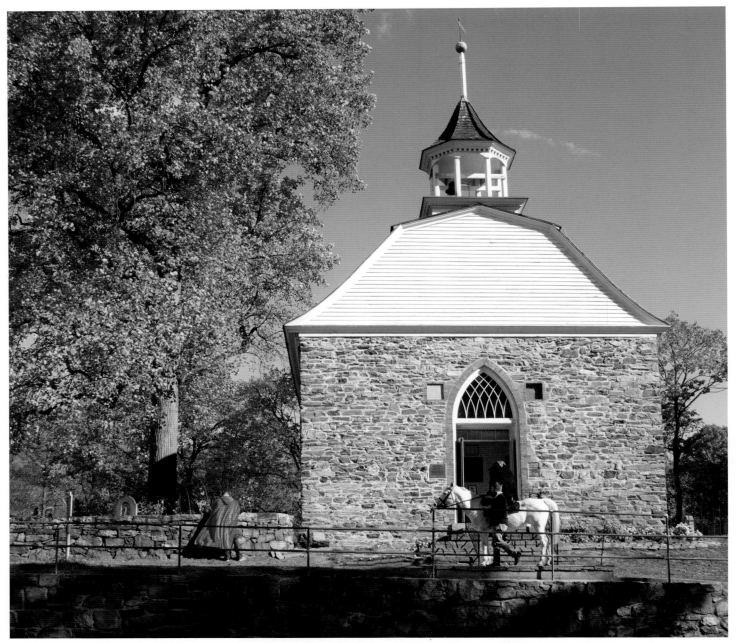

High Season. Thousands of visitors arrive in Sleepy Hollow each fall. Some even come in costume on Halloween! Previous page: Rev. Jeffrey Gargano baptizes Nicholas Arcigal, a descendant of Anna Lent, from one of the Old Dutch's earliest families. Photo: Family of Michael and Michelle Arcigal.

CELEBRATING 200 YEARS

"What influence has gone forth from the Philipse church of 1697!" exclaimed Rev. David Cole. It was a Monday afternoon in October 1897, and Cole was addressing an enormous crowd that had gathered to celebrate the 200th anniversary of the Old Dutch Church's formal organization. "Far reaching was the act of Domine Bertholf, which started your church life in 1697, and gave you your commission in the Master's Name. We of today can really see what was before him in hope only."

The two-day anniversary program of October 10–11 was one of the largest events Tarrytown had ever seen. The *New York Times* wrote that 40,000 visitors were expected. Theodore Roosevelt, who would become the 26th U.S. president in four years, agreed to make the keynote speech.

Long before October, the church began preparing for the festivities by taking steps to restore the building to its original appearance. Workers removed the false flat ceiling of 1837 and replaced hand-hewn beams behind it that were starting to decay. A new barrel ceiling of six-inch-wide oak planks was put in place to match the original. The plaster on the front walls of the apse, which had hidden the 45-degree corners, was taken back to the stone and replastered along the original lines. The changes re-created the fine acoustics of the original church.

The "modern" 1837 pulpit was removed. Alas, the original seventeenth-century pedestal pulpit was no longer available. Since only a handful of such pulpits existed in the East and none could be obtained, measurements were taken of the 1656 pulpit of the First Reformed Church of Albany, N.Y. That pulpit, saved when the original church was torn down, was believed to be similar to the original one in Sleepy Hollow. A replica was built and installed in the Old Dutch, along with stairs and a hexagonal sounding board. The spiffed-up church was ready to celebrate.

Favorable weather encouraged a large turnout for three services on Sunday and two on Monday. Among the notable speakers were Rev. John M. Ferris, who was pastor when the Second Reformed Church broke away from the Old Dutch Church a half-century earlier, and Rev. John B. Thompson, post–Civil War pastor of First Reformed. Ministers from other churches in Tarrytown also took part.

"THE PIOUS DEAD OF TWO CENTURIES CALL TO US FROM THESE VALLEYS AND HILLSIDES, WHERE THEY LABORED AND PRAYED SO LONG, TO PRESERVE, TRANSMIT AND EXTEND THE FAITH THEY PLANTED IN WEAKNESS AND WATERED WITH THEIR TEARS."

—REV. JOHN BODINE THOMPSON, 1897

Old Dutch in Postcards

New Bridge and Old Dutch Church, Tarrytown, N.Y.

OLD DUTCH CHURCH IN SLEEPY HOLLOW, TARRYTOWN, N. Y.   COPYRIGHT, 1903, BY DETROIT PHOTOGRAPHIC CO.

Author Hamilton W. Mabie spoke for all when he said, "Two hundred years ago … a lamp was lighted in the Old Dutch, and it has never gone out, nor burned more brightly than tonight."

On Monday evening, the main celebration was held at the 800-seat Tarrytown Music Hall. First Reformed's Rev. John Knox Allen introduced then-Assistant Secretary of the Navy Theodore Roosevelt. "I had to take the time and come speak at this two-hundredth anniversary of the founding of the Old Dutch Reformed Church," Roosevelt began. "For I have a certain ancestral connection with that church, to which for eight generations my people in this country have belonged."

He did not intend to speak only in praise of the Dutch "or merely in praise of us, their heirs," Roosevelt said. "The Dutch did great things in art, less in literature, and something in the sciences; they showed intellect in many ways. But it is not for that that we especially revere them. Intellect is a great thing. A sound mind is a great thing, just as a sound body is a great thing. But more than body and more than mind is what we call character. That is what counts ultimately with the individual and with the nation."

At the end of his speech, Roosevelt urged listeners, no matter their heritage, to "make up our minds that we will strive for the right as it is given to us to see the right; that we shall act as Americans and nothing else; and that we shall realize that in addition to the virtues needed in time of peace, we must be ever ready to display those virtues upon which call must always be made, should the time of peril again come to our common country."

BUILDING AT RISK!

Over the next decades, the Old Dutch Church sometimes seemed more museum than living church. Little use was made of the church in some years prior to the 1960s, when Rev. William Buitendorp started holding services there in July and August. In the mid-1970s, Rev. Gerald Vander Hart expanded use of the Old Dutch in summer, closing First Church at 242 North Broadway from June to September, for services at the old church. Christmas Eve services, Easter, Thanksgiving and various other events were added. And so it has continued ever since.

Throughout the century, the First Reformed consistory authorized repairs to the Old Dutch as needed—a new roof in 1939, paint and some new floor beams in 1946. The stone walls were repointed. Flat yellow bricks salvaged when the old windows were removed in 1837 were used to fill spaces in the walls, leaving some of the old bricks permanently in view. In the Burying Ground, volunteers reset headstones, filled in sunken graves and restored old paths.

National Historic Landmark. This plaque was installed on the front of the church in 1963.

In April 1962 came the good news: the National Park Service of the Department of the Interior had recently designated the building a National Historic Landmark.

By 1985, however, the Old Dutch Church was at another turning point in its long history. As in 1837, the structure had deteriorated so severely that collapse was a possibility. The culprit this time was not sun, rain and fire, but tiny beetles! By the time they were discovered, the half-inch-long powderpost beetles had eaten the belfry supports and part of the roof. Three structural roof timbers were unattached at one end, just hanging in midair. Both powderpost beetles and termites had also feasted on parts of the flooring and subfloor timbers, which enslaved Africans in the 1680s had laid directly on a dirt base. Window frames had deteriorated. Traffic vibrations from Route 9 had opened a crack in a masonry wall.

Back in 1837, $2,000 had covered the cost of major repairs and renovations. Although a lot of money at the time, it was quickly raised or borrowed. But in the 1980s, the cost of bringing the church back to its original condition had skyrocketed to more than $600,000! Few foundations made funds available to religious institutions, so the congregation turned to the community. A preservation committee of church members, led by Joanne and Vito Addotta and Rev. Vander Hart, threw themselves into a fund-raising effort, writing letters to corporations, giving interviews to media, organizing a fundraiser dinner, promoting an art exhibit about the church, staging readings of the "The Legend of Sleepy Hollow," and more. In a plea for community support, Joanne Addotta told a newspaper reporter in 1991, "The Old Dutch Church is not simply the possession of a small group of people. It is part of this community; it is the beginning of this community."

Contributions soon arrived from locals and indeed from around the United States; more than $225,000 was donated or raised via fundraisers. Help came from the state too. The church project became one of the first to benefit from a new Environmental Quality Bond Act to preserve buildings on the National Historic Landmark register—$120,000 in a matching grant. Bequests, endowments, interest and proceeds from the sale of church property topped up the fund. The big painted thermometer for donations, on a sign in front of the church, finally reached its target. Work began in 1991.

The goal was preservation, not simply restoration. Said Joanne Addotta, "We have an original building, an extant example of seventeenth-century Dutch colonial architecture, and we want to keep it the way it was." Carpenters replacing wood beams in the roof did not use nails but pegged mortise-and-tenon joints. Modern methods were used only where they did not detract from the authenticity of the building. The project was completed in three years. By 1994, the Old Dutch was back in business!

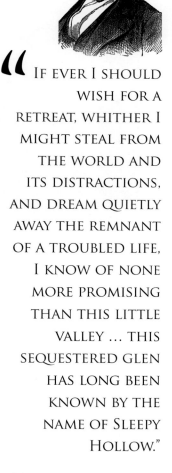

" IF EVER I SHOULD WISH FOR A RETREAT, WHITHER I MIGHT STEAL FROM THE WORLD AND ITS DISTRACTIONS, AND DREAM QUIETLY AWAY THE REMNANT OF A TROUBLED LIFE, I KNOW OF NONE MORE PROMISING THAN THIS LITTLE VALLEY ... THIS SEQUESTERED GLEN HAS LONG BEEN KNOWN BY THE NAME OF SLEEPY HOLLOW."

—WASHINGTON IRVING, "THE LEGEND OF SLEEPY HOLLOW," 1819–20

The Gold and Ivory Tablecloth

By Rev. Howard C. Schade

Pastor, First Church and Old Dutch Church, 1944-1951

At Christmas time men and women everywhere gather in their churches to wonder anew at the greatest miracle the world has ever known. But the story I like best to recall was not a miracle—not exactly.

It happened to a pastor who was very young. His church was very old. Once, long ago, it had flourished. Famous men had preached from its pulpit, prayed before its altar. Rich and poor alike had worshiped there and built it beautifully. Now the good days had passed from the section of town where it stood. But the pastor and his young wife believed in their run-down church. They felt that with paint, hammer and faith they could get it in shape. Together they went to work.

But late in December a severe storm whipped through the river valley, and the worst blow fell on the little church—a huge chunk of rain-soaked plaster fell out of the inside wall just behind the altar. Sorrowfully the pastor and his wife swept away the mess, but they couldn't hide the ragged hole.

The pastor looked at it and had to remind himself quickly, "Thy will be done!" But his wife wept, "Christmas is only two days away!"

That afternoon the dispirited couple attended an auction held for the benefit of a youth group. The auctioneer opened a box and shook out of its folds a handsome gold-and-ivory lace tablecloth. It was a magnificent item, nearly 15 feet long. But it, too, dated from a long-vanished era. Who, today, had any use for such a thing? There were a few halfhearted bids. Then the pastor was seized with what he thought was a great idea.

He bid it in for six dollars and fifty cents.

He carried the cloth back to the church and tacked it up on the wall behind the altar. It completely hid the hole! And the extraordinary beauty of its shimmering handwork cast a fine, holiday glow over the chancel. It was a great triumph. Happily he went back to preparing his Christmas sermon.

Just before noon on the day of Christmas Eve, as the pastor was opening the church, he noticed a woman standing in the cold at the bus stop.

"The bus won't be here for 40 minutes!" he called, and he invited her into the church to get warm.

She told him that she had come from the city that morning to be interviewed for a job as governess to the children of one of the wealthy families in town but she had been turned down. A war refugee, her English was imperfect.

The woman sat down in a pew and chafed her hands and rested. After a while she dropped her head and prayed. She looked up as the pastor began to adjust the great gold-and-ivory lace cloth across the hole. She rose suddenly and walked up the steps of the chancel. She looked at the tablecloth. The pastor smiled and started to tell her about the storm damage, but she didn't seem to listen. She took up a fold of the cloth and rubbed it between her fingers.

About the Author

Rev. Howard C. Schade became pastor of the First Reformed Church and the Old Dutch Church toward the end of World War II, in 1944. He continued his ministry in Sleepy Hollow for several years after the war. This story, published in Reader's Digest in December 1954, was very popular with readers and has been reprinted several times over the years. Was it inspired by an event that happened at Old Dutch or First Church? The answer is lost in time, but the article remains a poignant one.

"It is mine!" she said. "It is my banquet cloth!" She lifted up a corner and showed the surprised pastor that there were initials monogrammed on it. "My husband had the cloth made especially for me in Brussels! There could not be another like it!"

For the next few minutes the woman and the pastor talked excitedly together. She explained that she was Viennese; that she and her husband had opposed the Nazis and decided to leave the country. They were advised to go separately. Her husband put her on a train for Switzerland. They planned that he would join her as soon as he could arrange to ship their household goods across the border.

> " I HAVE ALWAYS FELT THAT IT WAS MY FAULT—TO LEAVE WITHOUT HIM," SHE SAID. "PERHAPS THESE YEARS OF WANDERING HAVE BEEN MY PUNISHMENT!"

She never saw him again. Later she heard that he had died in a concentration camp.

"I have always felt that it was my fault—to leave without him," she said. "Perhaps these years of wandering have been my punishment!"

The pastor tried to comfort her, urged her to take the cloth with her. She refused. Then she went away.

As the church began to fill on Christmas Eve, it was clear that the cloth was going to be a great success. It had been skillfully designed to look its best by candlelight.

After the service, the pastor stood at the doorway; many people told him that the church looked beautiful.

One gentle-faced, middle-aged man—he was the local clock-and-watch repairman—looked rather puzzled.

"It is strange," he said in his soft accent. "Many years ago my wife—God rest her—and I owned such a cloth. In our home in Vienna, my wife put it on the table"—and here he smiled—"only when the bishop came to dinner!"

The pastor suddenly became very excited. He told the jeweler about the woman who had been in church earlier in the day.

The startled jeweler clutched the pastor's arm. "Can it be? Does she live?"

Together the two got in touch with the family who had interviewed her. Then, in the pastor's car they started for the city. And as Christmas Day was born, this man and his wife—who had been separated through so many saddened Yuletides—were reunited.

To all who heard this story, the joyful purpose of the storm that had knocked a hole in the wall of the church was now quite clear. Of course people said it was a miracle, but I think you will agree it was the season for it!

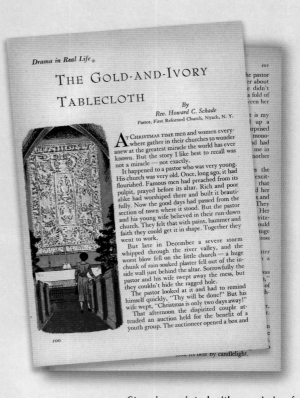

Music in the Air

By Rev. Gerald Vander Hart, pastor, 1972–1998

In its early years, music in the Old Dutch Church was unaccompanied. *Precentors*, or song leaders, led the congregation in singing. In later years, singers were accompanied by a viola or a harmonium. Over the 1970s and

Rev. and Mrs. Vander Hart

'80s, the church was used more frequently. Church member Bill Orser and I discussed installing a pipe organ in a Dutch-style case in the balcony. The dream was deferred when it became apparent in the 1990s that the church needed extensive restoration and preservation costing more than $600,000.

With the completion of the preservation project, Mr. and Mrs. Robert Newman donated $100,000 toward an organ. Almost $50,000 was raised by a committee headed by Barbara Vander Hart. Bill Orser had worked up a specification for the organ stops and the design of the casework enclosing the pipes and expressed a desire to build the organ. He received approval from the consistory in 1994. He and his father built the main case, but the inner works were more difficult than expected and funding was insufficient.

The consistory called a halt to Mr. Orser's work on the project in 1997 and authorized three organ firms to bid on completing the instrument. Fritz Noack of Georgetown, Mass., was awarded the contract. The tracker-action organ was inaugurated the next year with a recital by prominent organist Peter Sykes of Boston. At a dedication service on October 25, 1998, six months after our retirement, my wife Barbara, who had been choir director of the church, played the organ for the service. What a joy to hear the organ in worship!

Old Dutch Church organ, with detail view of the keys.
Photos at right: Jesse Rinka Photography.

REUNITED, AGAIN VIBRANT

The First and Second Reformed Churches remained on friendly terms and occasionally held joint services. At times Second Church would use Old Dutch for a worship service. Proposals to reunite the two churches were floated in 1914 and 1941, but did not succeed.

The two congregations flourished, with all-time membership highs in the 1950s and 1960s, but a slow decline developed in the 1970s. When Second Reformed Church's Rev. Lawrence Veenstra died suddenly in 1989, its consistory reopened a discussion with First Church, pastored by Rev. Gerald Vander Hart, about combining congregations. On December 2, 1990, large majorities in both congregations passed the proposal. The number of regular worshippers at Second Church was 130, First Church 100. The consistories retained the Old Dutch and Second Church buildings, as well as the parsonage in Philipse Manor. But the First Church building in North Tarrytown was sold to another Protestant congregation.

On January 27, 1991, Rev. Vander Hart preached his last sermon to a full house in First Church, where he had begun his Tarrytown ministry more than eighteen years before. He reviewed the building's history and its ties to the Old Dutch Church of Sleepy Hollow. "Like those who came here from the old church building," he said, "there is a continuity because the church is people—the people of Jesus Christ ... While we may not gather here, we will gather elsewhere and let's not forget elsewhere includes the old church."

An air of excitement took over a week later, when members of First Church, each wearing a name tag, entered Second Church in a group led by Rev. Vander Hart. Several carried the ancient artifacts of the Old Dutch Church, among them the 300-year-old silver baptismal bowl, and the silver beakers of Catherine and Frederick Philipse.

Some 140 years after breaking apart, the two congregations were again united. Rev. Vander Hart was installed as pastor, and the church was renamed the Reformed Church of the Tarrytowns. That June, as usual, the little church opened its doors, this time to a larger congregation.

Today the legendary Old Dutch Church of Sleepy Hollow is still vibrant, a place of holiness and history, of literature and culture. Each summer and at other special times of the year, its bronze bell—ringing now for more than three centuries, ringing, one hopes, for another three centuries—calls worshippers and visitors to its welcoming door!

" GRACIOUS GOD, WE ARE THE INHERITORS OF A LEGACY THAT OUR FOREBEARS COULD NOT HAVE IMAGINED. THROUGH YOUR BLESSINGS THESE PAST 300 YEARS, THIS CHURCH HAS BEEN KEPT AS A WITNESS TO YOUR FAITHFULNESS FROM GENERATION TO GENERATION. MAY YOUR PEOPLE IN YEARS TO COME EXPERIENCE YOUR LOVE AND PLACE THEIR TRUST IN YOU FOR THEIR LIFE AND DESTINY."

—PRAYER, PRESERVATION CELEBRATION SERVICE, JUNE 14, 1992

Evening of Music, Movie and Treats. Rev. Jeffrey Gargano welcomes everyone to the Dutch Treats reception.

CELEBRATING 325 YEARS

Post–Civil War Pastors at Old Dutch

1852–1866	*Abel T. Stewart*
1866–1869	*John Bodine Thompson*
1870–1920	*John Knox Allen*
1921–1930	*Walter A. Scholten*
1931–1940	*Robert T. Taylor*
1941–1943	*Duncan D. MacBryde*
1942–1944	*John W. Beardslee III*
1944–1951	*Howard C. Schade*
1952–1970	*William R. Buitendorp*
1972–1998	*Gerald Vander Hart*
1998–2000	*Don Peet*
2000–2007	*Michael Otte*
2007–2009	*William Doster*
2009–	*Jeffrey Gargano*

Another milestone: In 2010, the Old Dutch Church celebrated its 325th year. The kickoff event that spring was a "Dutch Treats" reception for the community. As the sun set over the Hudson and dusk settled over the churchyard, some 300 people were served refreshments and invited to view the *1715 First Record Book* on display. Later, many sat among the gravestones to watch the 1922 silent movie *The Headless Horseman*, projected onto a church wall. Once again hoofbeats echoed in the Burying Ground!

In the summer, an innovative music series called "Seven Sundays: A Celebration of Music in Worship" was introduced into worship. (It has since become an annual event.) Doors were opened to visitors on weekends, and a multimedia iPad tour was launched. A mere touch of the finger and 325 years of history came to life.

In October, the Old Dutch Gala included an organ concert by Kent Tritle, one of America's leading choral conductors and a renowned organist. "As we sat at the concert listening, the shadows gathering, the candles flickering, we could just feel the import of that wonderful, sacred, historic space," said Linda Knapp, who with her husband, Bob, was among the guests at the gala. "Truly magical!"

New milestones await the Old Dutch Church. Perhaps a lively celebration on its 400th anniversary, in 2085 ...

Making Old Dutch Accessible to Everyone

The Old Dutch Church draws visitors from around the world, yet for decades, access to this historic landmark was difficult for some because of the steep, uneven stone steps at the entrance. In 2016, the pastor, consistory and Friends of Old Dutch worked together on a plan for a more welcoming stairway, an expanded landing, a wheelchair ramp and paved paths in the churchyard. In the fall, they launched a $350,000 fundraising campaign with a generous bequest from the estate of Julia, Paul and John Vydareny. Construction began in March 2017 and was finished in June, in time for the summer worship season.

A New Day. Pastor Gargano greets church-goers at the new entrance (top); a ramp eases access for the elderly and disabled (bottom). Photos: Jesse Rinka Photography.

A New Tradition in Sleepy Hollow: Autumn Fest at the Old Dutch

When temperatures cool and trees start their fall color display, it's the signal for volunteers to converge on the Burying Ground to set up tents, tables, festive banners and displays for the annual Old Dutch Church Fest. This latest tradition, born in 2011 and held annually on October weekends ever since, has grown each year as Sleepy Hollow has become a favored Halloween destination. In 2016, an estimated 10,000 people came to the Fest over five weekends.

The attractions include a food tent, an Ale House, music, guided tours and visits by the Headless Horseman and Ichabod Crane. Master storyteller Jonathan Kruk performs his adaptation of *The Legend of Sleepy Hollow* in several sold-out performances. On Sundays in 2016, visitors were invited to join Rev. Gargano and a guest musician for a brief worship service in the church. A special worship service on Reformation Sunday closes out the Fest each year. Money raised in sales of food, beverages and souvenirs helps to offset maintenance and grounds-keeping expenses. In 2016 it also benefited the fundraising campaign for the Old Dutch Church Accessibility Project.

Many say fall is the most beautiful time of the year in the churchyard. When better to plan a visit to this National Historic Landmark?

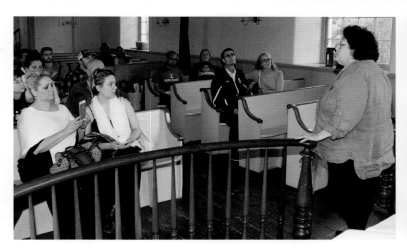

Autumn Fest. (Clockwise from top left) A child risks a peek at the Headless Horseman; Ichabod Crane makes an appearance; the grill crew takes a break; Pastor Jeff conducts the Blessing of the Horseman ceremony; the welcome sign is out; Deb tells visitors about the historic church, its legends and colorful characters; kids are keen to join the scavenger hunt; hotdogs are for sale, smiles are free.

121

PERSONAL NOTES

SELECTED BIBLIOGRAPHY

Allen, Rev. John Knox, D.D., "The Church in Westchester County," *Tercentenary Studies, 1928, a Record of Beginnings,* Reformed Church in America, 113–129.

———, *The Old Dutch Church of Sleepy Hollow with the Story of Jacob the Roman,* Tarrytown (N.Y.) Historical Society, 1918.

Allen, Thomas B., *Tories: Fighting for the King in America's First Civil War,* New York: Harper Collins, 2010.

American Scenic & Historic Preservation Society, *13th Annual Report to the Legislature of the State of New York,* Albany: J. B. Lyon, 1908.

Bacon, Clarence E., "Annals of the First Reformed Church of Tarrytown," *240th Anniversary 1697–1937,* First Reformed Church.

Bacon, Edgar Mayhew, *Chronicles of Tarrytown and Sleepy Hollow,* New York: G. P. Putnam's Sons, 1897.

———, comp., *First English Record Book of the Dutch Reformed Church in Sleepy Hollow,* Tarrytown (N.Y.) Historical Society, 1931.

Bailey, Rosalie Fellows, *Pre-Revolutionary Dutch Houses and Families in Northern New Jersey and Southern New York,* New York: William Morrow, 1936.

Bolton, Robert, *The History of Several Towns, Manors and Patents of the County of Westchester from Its First Settlement to the Present Time,* New York: Alexander S. Gould, 1848, 1881, 1905.

Bradshaw, Elinor R., "Philipsburgh Manor at North Tarrytown, N.Y.," *Halve-Maen* (October 1969 and January 1970).

Brooks, Van Wyck, *The World of Washington Irving,* New York: Putnam, 1944.

Brouwer, Arie R., *Reformed Church Roots,* Reformed Church Press, 1977.

Burstein, Andrew, *The Original Knickerbocker: The Life of Washington Irving,* Basic Books, 2007.

Butler, Joseph T., *Sleepy Hollow Restorations: A Cross-Section of the Collection,* Tarrytown, N.Y.: Sleepy Hollow Restorations Inc., 1983.

Canning, Jeff, and Wally Buxton, *History of the Tarrytowns,* Harrison, N.Y.: Harbor Hill Books, 1975.

Centennial of the Theological Seminary of the Reformed Church in America, 1784–1884, New York: Board of Publications of the RCA, 1885.

Cole, Rev. David, D.D., translator, *First Record Book of the Old Dutch Church of Philipsburg Manor,* Yonkers Historical and Library Association, Yonkers, N.Y., 1901.

Conklin, Margaret Swancott, *Historical Tarrytown & North Tarrytown (a Guide),* Tarrytown (N.Y.) Historical Society, 1939.

Corwin, Charles E., "Incidents of Reformed Church Life in New York During the Revolutionary War," *Journal of the Presbyterian Historical Society,* 1917–1918, vol. 9, 355–367.

———, *A Manual of the Reformed Church in America, 1628–1922,* New York: Board of Publication of the Reformed Church in America, 1922.

Corwin, Edward Tanjore, *A Manual of the Reformed Church in America, 1628–1902,* 4th ed., Board of Publication of the Reformed Church in America, N.Y., 1902.

Countryman, Edward, *A People in Revolution,* Baltimore: Johns Hopkins University Press, 1981.

Cushman, Elisabeth, *Historic Westchester, 1683–1933,* Westchester County Historical Society, 1933.

De Jong, Gerald Francis, "The Dutch Reformed Church and Negro Slavery in Colonial America," *Church History,* vol. 40, no. 4 (December 1971), 423–436.

Documents of the Assembly of the State of New York, 130th Session, 1907, vol. 30, no. 70, Albany, N.Y.: J. B. Lyon, 1907.

Dwight, Timothy, LL.D., *Travels in New-England and New-York,* New Haven, Conn.: A. Converse, 1821.

Earle, Alice Morse, *Colonial Days in Old New York,* New York: Charles Scribner's Sons, 1896.

———, *Home Life in Colonial Days,* New York: Macmillan, 1898; reprinted by Jonathan David Publishers, 1975.

Ecclesiastical Records, State of New York, Albany, N.Y.: J. B. Lyon, 1902, 1905.

Fabend, Firth Haring, *A Dutch Family in the Middle Colonies, 1660–1800,* New Brunswick, N.J.: Rutgers University Press, 1991.

Hageman, Howard G., Rev. Dr., "Colonial New Jersey's First Domine: II," *Halve-Maen* (October 1969 and January 1970).

———, "The Dutch Battle for Higher Education in the Middle Colonies," *A Beautiful and Fruitful Place, Selected Rensselaerswijck Seminar Papers,* New Netherland Project, 1991.

Hall, Edward Hagaman, L.H.D, "The Manor of Philipsborough," address written for the New York Branch of the Order of Colonial Lords of Manors in America, www.rootsweb.ancestry.com/~nywestch/manors/philipse2.htm.

Harland, Marion, *Some Colonial Homesteads and Their Stories,* New York: G. P. Putnam's Sons, 1900.

Heaton, Major Basil, *A Short History of Rhual,* Shrewsbury (England): Livesey, 1987.

Hill, David Jayne, *Washington Irving,* New York: Sheldon, 1879.

Historic Hudson Valley, www.hudsonvalley.org.

Horne, Philip Field, *A Land of Peace: The Early History of Sparta, a Landing Town on the Hudson,* Ossining, N.Y.: Ossining Restoration Committee, 1976.

———, Research Report 1–28, Sleepy Hollow Restorations, Tarrytown, N.Y., Aug. 1976–July 1977.

Hufeland, Otto, *Westchester County During the American Revolution, 1775–1783,* Harrison, N.Y.: Harbor Hill Books, 1974.

Hutchinson, Lucille and Theodore, *The Centennial History of North Tarrytown,* 1974.

Images of Tarrytown and Sleepy Hollow, published by The Historical Society, Inc., Arcadia, 1997.

Irving, Pierre M., *Life and Letters of Washington Irving,* New York: G. P. Putnam and Sons, 1883.

Irving, Washington, *George Washington, A Biography,* abridged and edited by Charles Neider, De Capo Press edition 1994.

———, *Rip Van Winkle & The Legend of Sleepy Hollow,* Tarrytown, N.Y.: Sleepy Hollow Restorations, 1974.

———, "Sleepy Hollow," introduction by Henry Steiner, Sleepy Hollow, N.Y.: Sleepy Hollow Publishing, 1996 (www.sleepyhollowny.gov).

————, *Wolfert's Roost,* New York: G. P. Putnam and Son, 1868.

Joby, Christopher Richard, *Calvinism and the Arts: A Re-assessment,* Leuven, Belgium: Peeters, 2007.

Johnson, Kathleen Eagen, *Van Cortlandt Manor,* Historic Hudson Valley Press, 1997.

Knickerbocker, New York Monthly Magazine, August 1840.

Knower, Daniel, Dr., "Historical Address," *Ceremonies on Laying Cornerstone of David Williams' Monument, Sept. 23, 1876, at Schoharie,* Albany, N.Y.: Weed, Parsons, 1876, 67–80.

Longfellow, Henry, "Address on the Death of Washington Irving," *Poems and Other Writings* (J. D. McClatchy, ed.), Library of America, 2000.

Lossing, Benson J., *The Hudson, From the Wilderness to the Sea,* Troy, N.Y.: H. B. Nims, 1866.

————, *Pictorial Field-Book of the Revolution,* vol. 2, New York: Harper & Brothers, 1859.

Mackenzie, Grenville C., "The Early Settlement of Philipsburg," *The Quarterly Bulletin of the Westchester County Historical Society,* White Plains, N.Y. , vol. 12, no. 4, October 1936; also see two inserts: "Contributed Notes."

————, "The Old Sleepy Hollow Cemetery," *The Quarterly Bulletin of the Westchester County Historical Society,* White Plains, N.Y. , vol. 16, no. 2, April 1940.

————, *Families of the Colonial Town of Philipsburgh,* 1966, reference copy: Westchester County Historical Society.

Maika, Dennis J., "Commerce and Community: Manhattan Merchants in the Seventeenth Century," dissertation submitted to New York University, May 1995.

————, "The Commercial Career of Frederick Philipse," prepared for Historic Hudson Valley, October 1996.

————, "Encounters: Slavery and the Philipse Family 1680–1751," *Dutch New York: The Roots of Hudson Valley Culture* (Roger Panetta, ed.), Hudson River Museum, Fordham University Press, 2009, 35–72.

Malone, Duman, ed., *Dictionary of American Biography,* vol. 3, New York: Charles Scribner's Sons, 1934.

Manderen, Carl, "The Old Dutch Church of Sleepy Hollow 1837–1874," address to First Reformed Church, North Tarrytown, May 19, 1974.

McCoy, Faye Bertholf, *The Bertholf Story,* 1977.

Morrison, Hugh, *Early American Architecture From the First Colonial Settlements to the National Period,* New York: Oxford University Press, 1952.

Myers, Andrew B., *The Worlds of Washington Irving 1783–1859,* Tarrytown, N.Y.: Sleepy Hollow Restorations, 1974.

Nelson, Paul David, *William Tryon and the Course of Empire: A Life in British Imperial Service,* University of North Carolina Press, 1990.

The Old Dutch Burying Ground of Sleepy Hollow, History Research Society of the Tappan Zee, New York: Montague Lee, 1926.

Owens, William A., *Pocantico Hills 1609–1959,* Tarrytown, N.Y.: Sleepy Hollow Restorations, 1960.

Perry, William, *The Old Dutch Burying Ground of Sleepy Hollow in North Tarrytown, N.Y., a Record of the Early Gravestones and Their Inscriptions,* Boston: Rand Press, 1953.

Raftery, Patrick, *The Cemeteries of Westchester County,* Elmsford, N.Y.: Westchester County Historical Society, 2011.

Raymond, Marcius D., comp., *Souvenir of the Revolutionary Soldiers' Monument Dedication at Tarrytown, N.Y.,* Tarrytown: Roger Sherwood Printers, 1894.

Reflections of Faith: Religious Folk Art in America, Museum of American Folk Art, December 9, 1983–January 21, 1984.

Reynolds, Helen Wilkinson, *Dutch Houses in the Hudson Valley Before 1776,* Holland Society of New York, 1929, republished by Dover Publications, 1965.

Scharf, J. Thomas, *History of Westchester County,* New York: L. E. Preston, 1886.

Shonnard, Frederick, and W. W. Spooner, *History of Westchester County: From Its Earliest Settlement to the Year 1900,* New York: New York History Co., 1900, reprinted by Harbor Hill Books, New York, 1974.

Sparling, Reed, *Hudson Valley Voyage: Through the Seasons, Through the Years,* Involvement Media, Inc., 2007.

Spooner, William, *Westchester County, New York, Biographical,* New York: New York History Co., 1900.

Steiner, Henry, Introduction to Washington Irving's "Sleepy Hollow," Sleepy Hollow Publishing, 1996 (www.sleepyhollowny.gov).

————, *The Place Names of Historic Sleepy Hollow and Tarrytown,* Westminster, Md.: Heritage Books, 2008.

Stewart, Abel T., *Historical Discourse,* First Reformed Church of North Tarrytown, 1866.

Tales of the Old Dutch Burying Ground, Friends of the Old Dutch Burying Ground, (3rd ed.), Bridgeport , Conn.: Alliance Printing Group, 2006.

Todd, Rev. John A., "On the Character and Death of Washington Irving," *National Preacher,* vol. 33, issue no. 1.

Two Hundredth Anniversary of the Old Dutch Church at Sleepy Hollow, 1697–1897, Consistory of the First Reformed Church of Tarrytown, Tarrytown, N.Y.: De Vinne Press, 1898.

Veit, Richard Frances, and Mark Nonestied, *New Jersey Cemeteries and Tombstones: History in the Landscape,* New Brunswick, N. J.: Rivergate Books, 2008.

Vetare, Margaret L., *Philipsburg Manor Upper Mills,* Historic Hudson Valley Press, 2004.

Warner, Charles Dudley, *Washington Irving,* New York: Houghton, Mifflin, 1884.

Weintraub, Stanley, *General Washington's Christmas Farewell, a Mount Vernon Homecoming, 1783,* New York: Free Press, 2003.

Williams, Gray, *Picturing Our Past: National Register Sites in Westchester County,* Elmsford, N.Y.: Westchester County Historical Society, 2003.

————, "Solomon Brewer: A Connecticut Valley Yankee in Westchester County," Markers XI, *Journal of the Association for Gravestone Studies,* (Richard E. Meyer, ed.), 1994.

NOTES

Major reference sources are church files and the following books:
Edgar Mayhew Bacon, *First English Record Book of the Dutch Reformed Church of Sleepy Hollow*, 1931; Rev. David Cole, *First Record Book of the Old Dutch Church of Sleepy Hollow*, 1901; *Tales of the Old Dutch Burying Ground*, 2006; *The Old Dutch Burying Ground of Sleepy Hollow*, 1926; William Perry, *The Old Dutch Burying Ground of Sleepy Hollow in North Tarrytown*, 1953; Rev. John Knox Allen, *The Old Dutch Church of Sleepy Hollow with the Story of Jacob the Roman*, 1918; and *Two Hundredth Anniversary of the Old Dutch Church at Sleepy Hollow 1697–1897*, 1898.

The following notes highlight selected additional resources.

PREFACE
Page viii: *New York's oldest church.* Frederick Philipse started construction of the church in 1684. The year 1685, engraved on its bell (cast in Holland), is used as the church's completion date. While other places of worship in New York started prior to Philipse's church, such as the Old Dutch Church in Kingston, organized in 1659, the original church buildings no longer exist. In New York City, for instance, St. Paul's Chapel, which opened in 1766, is "Manhattan's oldest public building in continuous use." A Reformed Church of America (RCA) publication identifies the Old Dutch Church of Sleepy Hollow as the oldest RCA church building still in use.
Sources: Canning, *History*, 26; *Tales*, 13, 18; *Images of Tarrytown*, 107; Hutchinson, *Centennial*, 16; Allen, *The Old Dutch Church of Sleepy Hollow*; *The Old Dutch Burying Ground of Sleepy Hollow, 1926*, 8; *Church Herald* Anniversary issue, April 7, 1978, Reformed Church of America; and Bolton, *The History of Several Towns*, 1905, 526. Websites: www.nps.gov/nhl/, trinitywallstreet.org, olddutchchurch.org, stpeterschurchalbany.org.

CHAPTER 1
Page 8
1961: National Historic Landmark: The National Park Service (www.nps.gov) designated the Old Dutch a historic landmark on November 5, 1961, although the plaque near the door states 1963, when the plaque was installed.

CHAPTER 2
Page 11
10 fathoms of duffils ... 70 fathoms of wampum: Bolton, *History of Several Towns*, vol. 1, 1848, 175–176.
Philipse speculated ... in his cellars: American Scenic & Historic, 183.
Now Philipse followed the Pocantico ... farmers earlier in the century: from *Two Hundredth Anniversary* (Rev. David Cole), 122; also, Grenville Mackenzie, "Early Settlement," 86.
Page 12
Philipse's origins were modest ... continued the family business: letters from C. R. Schriek, researcher in the Netherlands, to First Church's Rev. Gerald Vander Hart, March 27 and Nov. 7, 1991.
so in 1653 ... master carpenter: Vetare, *Upper Mills*, 19.
Claiming the small burgherright ... from the municipal government, Maika, "Commerce and Community," 196.
Page 13
The Land Barons: Today the Manor would be worth ... acre in 2011: www.landandfarm.com.
In all ... more than 50,000 acres: Vetare, *Upper Mills*, 19. The acreage has varied over the years to as much as 92,000. Most recent calculations are closer to 57,000 (Vetare, note, 60).
Page 15
By 1697, there were ... former New Netherland colony: from *Two Hundredth Anniversary*, 126–7.
The Philipses wanted a Reformed minister ... "but he organized it," wrote Rev. Cole: Cole, *200th Anniversary*, 127–128.
Philipse, a former carpenter ... in the seventeenth century: Fabend, *A Dutch Family*. Octagonal churches were built in Flatbush in 1663, Bergen in 1680, Hackensack in 1696, New Utrecht in 1700, Bushwick in 1705, 153.
Note Exmorra's steep-pitched roof ... Hudson Valley until the 1720s.: Reynolds, in *Dutch Houses in the Hudson Valley* (p. 23), wrote that the gambrel was popular in the Hudson Valley between 1725 and 1775; Morrison, *Early American Architecture* (pp.116, 120), writes that the gambrel roof on Flemish colonial houses was an eighteenth-century style, popular starting in 1725.

That was when the steep-pitched roof on the Upper Mills ... with a gambrel: Robert Yasinsac, Philipsburg Manor Site Manager.
... mortared them into place using ... make it more durable: Reynolds, *Dutch Houses*, 18.
(Caption) For the windows ... in the belfry: "The Old Dutch Church as It Used to Look," *Chronicle of the Historical Society of the Tarrytowns*, May 1963, no. 15, 3. The illustration is by David M. Clarke, who was an elder of the First Reformed Church of North Tarrytown.
Page 16
Of Noble Birth? For example, Westchester County ... "name and country": Bolton, *The History of Several Towns*, New York, vol. 1, 1881, 508.
Of Noble Birth? Contrary to Bolton's ... as early as 1581: letter from researcher C. R. Schriek to First Church's Rev. Gerald Vander Hart, Nov. 7, 1991. Also see Horne, Sleepy Hollow Restorations report, 1–28.
"Because the Dutch ... in the Netherlands,": De Jong, "The Dutch Reformed Church and Negro Slavery," 424. The first black slaves arrived at New Amsterdam about 1626, wrote De Jong (p. 423).
Even churchmen ... evil of slavery: ibid., 424.
At least one church even owned ... signed the consistory's document: *Ecclesiastical Records, State of New York*, 1905, VI: 4184.
"In 1685, Philipse's ship the Charles *... in Philipse's Manhattan household."*: Maika, "Encounters," 39.
Page 18
Roof: Flaring eaves are thought to be of Flemish origin, from the maritime region of Flanders (southern Holland, western Belgium, northern tip of France), Morrison, *Early American Architecture*, 119.
Gambrel: see notes for page 15.
Walls: Hudson River mud, mixed ... seal the joints: Morrison, *Early American Architecture*, 102.
1685 Bell: Bell founder Gerhard Schimmel is named as the maker in a letter from the Carillon Museum in Asten, Holland, to William Lent at the Reformed Church of the Tarrytowns, Apr. 28, 1992.
Page 20
He Spelled It How? "The weather vane still displays ... changed to F.F. or F.P.": Edgar Mayhew Bacon, "A Notable Anniversary," Tarrytown Historical Society files.
One Sleepy Hollow Restorations researcher ... Philipse's name: Bradshaw, "Philipsburgh Manor," *Halve-Maen*, October 1969, 7.
"In the hundreds of times ... 'Frederick Vlypson'": Horne, Sleepy Hollow Restorations report 1–28, 3.
The Ladies of the Church. "Capable, but not ... very cultivated": Allen, "Church in Westchester," Tercentenary Studies, 118
Page 21
"Rev. Allen described ... "charming manners": ibid., 118
Historian Robert Bolton ... building of the church: Bolton, *The History of Several Towns*, vol. 1, 1881, 529.
But she did take ... searching for a minister: Cole, *Two Hundredth Anniversary*.
Philipse & Capt. Kidd. Harland, *Colonial Homesteads*, 243–249, tells the story of Philipse's suspected connections with the pirate Kidd. Also see a biographical sketch of Philipse in Malone's *Dictionary of American Biography*.
Page 22
Specifically, Calvin opposed most ... to psalm singing: Joby, *Calvinism and the Arts*, 3, 73.
Attention should be on the preaching, Morrison, *Early American Architecture*, 117.
Communion Table: given to the church sometime after 1692: Butler, Sleepy Hollow Restorations, 61.

CHAPTER 3
Page 27
It is unknown if the few ... 1680s and 1690s: Mackenzie, "Early Settlement," *Quarterly Bulletin*, October 1936, 86.
By 1697 there were about twenty poor ... living on Philipsburg Manor: Earl of Bellomont, governor of New York, Jan. 2, 1701, letter to the Council of Trade and Plantations.

Pages 28-30
Many of the family details in "The Settlers" appeared in two publications by Grenville C. Mackenzie: "The Early Settlement of Philipsburg" (including

corrections printed on two loose inserts), in *Quarterly Bulletin,* October 1936; and *Families of the Colonial Town of Philipsburgh,* Westport, Conn., 1966, reference copy available at Westchester County Historical Society.

Page 30

Carel Davids was … eleven children: Horne, *Land of Peace,* 8–9.

Philipsburg Rents: The first settlers … Philipse's gristmill and sawmill; also *In the early days … farm laborer:* ibid., 6, 7 & 9.

Philipsburg Rents: They could … sale price, Steiner, *Place Names,* 100.

Page 31

First baptisms April 21, 1697: Cole, *First Record Book,* 23. The baptisms register (see photo, p. 39) appears to show the date April 21, 1696. The Cole translation has April 21, 1697.

Pages 31–32

What a colorful display… kept in order by the choir leader: condensed from EM Bacon, *Chronicles of Tarrytown and Sleepy Hollow,* 1897, 41–44.

Page 32

Did the Enslaved Africans Join the Church? In the early eighteenth … to become members: Maika, "Encounters," 46.

Pages 32-33

In the typical fashion of the day … "was without a copy.": Fabend, *A Dutch Family,* 154-155.

Page 34

"That such a perilous passage was taken … satisfy it": ibid., 157.

Page 35

Pietists disdained what they called … mother church in Amsterdam: Hageman, "Colonial New Jersey's First Domine: II," *Halve-Maen,* January 1970, 18.

Ministers who "chatter to the Lord in a cold voice." Fabend, in *A Dutch Family,* p. 154, attributes the quote to Willem Schortinguis, a Dutch Pietist. *Adherents of Pietism … truly be saved,* Fabend, *A Dutch Family,* 138–139.

"Certain men came over … liturgy": letter from Rev. Henry Selyns to the Classis of Amsterdam, Sept. 20, 1685, *Ecclesiastical Records, State of New York,* 1901, II: 907.

Page 36

In 1692, one Albany and two New York … "without ministers or sacraments": letter from Revs. Selyns, Varick and Dellius, Oct. 12, 1692, *Ecclesiastical Records, State of New York,* 1901, II: 1043.

"Independent and adventurous … cooperation, and order": Fabend, *A Dutch Family,* 157.

Rev. David Cole, First Record Book … "capacity for teaching": from *Two Hundredth Anniversary,* 129.

"So godly was his life … the denomination": attributed by Faye Bertholf McCoy to New York Genealogical Society records, *The Bertholf Story,* 1977, 23.

Page 37

"Although he built … saintly," Allen, "Church in Westchester," *Tercentenary Studies,* 118.

"I bequeath … purpose whatsoever: Bradshaw, "Philipsburgh Manor," *Halve-Maen,* January 1970, 15.

Page 40

One writer compared a tax list … church was thriving, Horne, *Land of Peace,* 8–9.

Page 40-41

By 1755, discussions over American … proposal that didn't go anywhere, C. E. Corwin, *Manual of the Reformed Church,* New York, 1922, 62–63; also see Hageman, "Dutch Battle for Higher Education," 39.

Page 41

"Rev. Ritzema, at this time … friend of the English": Bolton, *The History of Several Towns,* vol. 1, 1848, 336.

(Caption) no more than 100 members lived … including 39 enslaved Africans: Mackenzie, "Early Settlement," 86, 88.

(Caption) Before the Revolution … 1,100 to 1,500 people: Countryman, *People in Revolution,* 17.

CHAPTER 4

Page 45-46

The earliest pioneer burials … before 1700: Shonnard and Spooner, *History of Westchester County,* 161.

Page 46

A first-person account … fifties: Raftery, *Cemeteries of Westchester County,* 98.

Page 47

With increased prosperity … sandstone markers: Mackenzie, "The Old Sleepy Hollow Cemetery," 32.

The use of this easy-to-carve … artistic gravestones: Williams, "Solomon Brewer," 52–81.

By the Numbers … 11 stones in Dutch: Perry, *Old Dutch Burying Ground* (1953) and *Quarterly Bulletin,* vol. 16, April 1940, 34.

By the Numbers … 3,193 estimated interments up to 1885: Allen, *Old Dutch Church of Sleepy Hollow,* 26, and Raftery, *Cemeteries of Westchester County,* 98. 180 burials before 1,700 + 1,073 (1700s) + 1,940 (1800s) = 3,193.

By the Numbers … 76 soldiers: from Raymond, *Souvenir of the Revolutionary Soldiers:* 21.

By the Numbers … 281 estimated number of stones by Brewer: Williams, "Solomon Brewer," 78, 79. Brewer has 223 surviving stones at Old Dutch as well as 45 (gone) and 13 (commissioned in Brewer's book, but not recorded at Old Dutch) = 281.

Page 48

The final resting place … "be there": Todd, "Character and Death of Washington Irving," 20–28.

All of the seventy-six soldiers: from Raymond, *Souvenir of the Revolutionary Soldiers,* 21.

Page 49

Soon, with space for … (1,073 and 1,940 burials): Raftery, *Cemeteries of Westchester County,* 98.

Page 50

At the Old Dutch Church … still grace the graveyard": Williams, "Solomon Brewer, 78–79.

Page 52

During the Revolution … Rockland County: Veit and Nonestied, *New Jersey Cemeteries,* 62.

Page 53

Early records indicated … "to the grave": from Raymond, *Souvenir of the Revolutionary Soldiers,* 109.

Page 54

Rev. John M. Ferris … "they knew": from *Two Hundredth Anniversary,* 63.

Page 56

Arise, Ye Dead! … "call up the rest": Allen, *Old Dutch Church of Sleepy Hollow,* 27.

Page 57

What Lies Beneath? … "occupation": ibid., 20–21.

Love Eternal … Frena: Tales of the Old Dutch, 36, 37.

CHAPTER 5

Page 61

"No part of the country … foe alike": E. M. Bacon quotes Irving in *Chronicles of Tarrytown,* 71.

Many Westchester farmers … the British: Hufeland, *Westchester County,* 74–5.

"The controversy between England and … confined to a very few": ibid., *Westchester County,* 10.

Most Philipsburg Manor tenants had not … 15 percent were revolutionary: Countryman, *People in Revolution,* 119.

"the more affluent were more … become Whigs, or Patriots": Henry Steiner; also see Countryman, *People in Revolution,* 120.

In 1775 the Continental Congress … loyalists under control: Hufeland, *Westchester County,* 66–7.

One of Hammond's early challenges was laxness … "Congress will immediately put the men under pay": ibid., 75.

Page 62

But the men's enthusiasm flagged … take care of their harvests: ibid., 75.

In time the farmers' "obstinate … with force": Scharf, *History of Westchester,* 198.

Pages 62-63

"When the war … so large a number of heroes": E. M. Bacon, *Chronicles of Tarrytown,* 71–72, 74.

Page 63

This led … safekeeping: New York Harbor Parks, www.nyharborparks.org.

British troops burned … independence: Old Dutch Church, Kingston, www.olddutchchurch.org/museum.php.

Under Gov. William … burned parts of Tarrytown, Nelson, *William Tryon,* 157–158.

Page 64

Bullet Holes? … a repairman at work … the Revolution: from *New York Times,* "225th Anniversary Services at Sleepy Hollow Church," Oct. 15, 1922.

Page 65

John Jay, the first … favor the Loyalists, American Scenic & Historic, 1908, 205.

"We are determined at the hazard ... king and constitution": Scharf, *History of Westchester*, vol. 1, 248.

Pages 66–67

Hand of God Intervenes: Main sources: Affadavits of John Paulding (May 1817) and Isaac Van Wart (January 1817), and autobiography of David Williams; and Dr. Daniel Knower, "Historical Address," all published in *Ceremonies on Laying Cornerstone of David Williams' Monument at Schoharie Court House, Sept. 23, 1876*, 49–54 (see Knower in Bibliography).

Page 67

The astonishing event ... Washington called it, Ronald Mann, National Center for Constitutional Studies, January 2004, www.nccs.net/newsletter/jan04nl.html.

Frena Romer's Bowl, Henry Steiner, excerpt from "A Very Hot Whig," © Henry John Steiner.

Page 68

The general ordered a halt ... until nightfall: George Washington's diary entry for July 2, 1781: "At three o'clock this Morning I commenced my March with the Continental Army in order to cover the detached Troops and improve any advantages which might be gained by them. Made a small halt at the New bridge over Croton abt. 9 Miles from Peekskill—another at the Church by Tarry Town till Dusk." *George Washington Diary*, Library of Congress.

Romance Nipped in the Bud? Unlikely, says Washington ... Morris was courting Miss Philipse: Irving, *George Washington*, 83–84.

Page 69

Continentals, "ill-clad and weather-beaten," Weintraub, *Christmas Farewell*, 52.

Page 70

"He was compensated ... for those times": Heaton, *A Short History of Rhual*, 16.

"He died in 1785 ... stage of life": Bolton, *The History of Several Towns*, vol. 1, 1881, 524.

Page 71

The last veteran of that war was laid to rest ... November 1851: from *Souvenir of the Revolutionary Soldiers*, 108.

"They were noble men ... deemed to be their duty": from Raymond, *Souvenir of the Revolutionary Soldiers*, 19, 21.

Page 72

"The stout Jacob ... no trace behind": ibid., 117.

It was confirmed ... pension application: ibid., 120–121.

Page 73

Luck or Destiny?: While still a teenager ... silver sleeve buttons: ibid., 60.

Page 74

Abraham Martling (d.1786) a daredevil ... one published report: John P. Ritter, "Heroes of the Neutral Ground," *Frank Leslie's Popular Monthly*, July 1897, 6.

Martling had once caused Underhill's arrest, Shonnard and Spooner, *History*, 459; *The Old Dutch Burying Ground of Sleepy Hollow*, 1926, 46–47.

Page 75

Concealed on the side ... confiscated Philipsburg Manor: from Raymond, *Souvenir of the Revolutionary Soldiers*, 186.

On April 13, 1775, at the request ... support to the king: Bolton, *The History of Several Towns*, vol. 2, 1848, 352.

Page 76

Joseph Youngs: See E. M. Bacon, *Chronicles of Tarrytown*, 81, and Raymond, *Souvenir of the Revolutionary Soldiers*, 198–200.

Westchester Guides: Lieutenant Odell himself ... for his capture": from Raymond, *Souvenir of the Revolutionary Soldiers*, 82.

Westchester Guides: John Odell's foray to Delancey's house: Hufeland, *Westchester County*, 433.

CHAPTER 6
Page 79

"Think of the innate love ... all around him": Washington Irving; Commemoration of the One Hundredth Anniversary of His Birth," Washington Irving Association at Tarrytown-on-Hudson, April 3, 1883, 32.

Once as a young boy ... gave his blessing: "Irving Turned from Law to Literary Career That Brought Him Fame," *Daily News*, January 27, 1940; Joseph T. Butler, "Historic Sunnyside," Historic Hudson Valley (www.hudsonvalley.org).

Page 80

And the Pauldings' cousin John ... the Revolutionary War: Burstein, *Original Knickerbocker*, 11, and "Irving Turned from Law to Literary Career," *Daily News*, January 27, 1940.

The Church, as Irving ... "wide neighborhood": Irving, "Sleepy Hollow,"

1839.

Something in the Air ... 1928: Allen, "Church in Westchester," 128.

Page 81

"My spirits are very unequal ... of my friends": Pierre M. Irving, *The Life and Letters of Washington Irving*, 343–345.

Irving sent his brother ... " manners, etc.": ibid., 374.

The sketch "touched ... the present legend: ibid., 374.

Page 82

"The church gains ... romance about it": from *Two Hundredth Anniversary*, 6.

In an article ... prestigious organization," Joseph T. Butler, "Washington Irving, Squire of Sunnyside," Historic Hudson Valley (www.hudsonvalley.org)

Glory Be to God ...'" lifted up'": Hill, *Washington Irving*, 176.

Page 82-83

"There was no man ... and France": letter from Mrs. Jack Dorland, president, Potpourri Garden Club of Westchester, to Lemuel A. Garrison, U.S. Department of the Interior, National Park Service, 8/8/69, requesting National Historic Landmark designation for the Old Dutch.

Page 83

Soon Irving embellished ... "an old cocked hat": Kenneth S. Lynn, "Washington Irving Saw the American Past—Sunnyside Up," *Smithsonian*, August 1983, 94.

This home was ... "a little paradise": from "Washington Irving's Sunnyside," Historic Hudson Valley (www.hudsonvalley.org).

That country's political unrest ... wished them to be: Irving, *The Life and Letters of Washington Irving*, 74.

Irving never married ... for the rest of his life: Warner, *Washington Irving*, 60.

Did Irving Attend the Old Dutch?: Earle Parker O'Brien, "Christ Church Cherishes Links to Washington Irving, the Churchman," *Daily News*, January 27, 1940, no. 23, second section.

Page 84

"When Washington Irving died ... Cemetery": Henry Steiner, "The Last Days of Washington Irving," *River Journal*, November 29, 1999.

Page 84-85

"The funeral route ... like Irving": Betty Dorland, "Thousands Attended Tarrytown Funeral of Irving," *Daily News*, Tarrytown, N.Y., November 27, 1968, 9.

Page 85

After Irving's death ... "History of Letters": Longfellow, "Address on the Death of Washington Irving."

Final Resting Place ... "boyhood": Pierre M. Irving, *Life and Letters of Washington Irving*, 184.

Instead, he eventually settled ... "bones there": Sleepy Hollow Cemetery (www.sleepyhollowcemetery.org).

Page 90

Daniel Van Tassel, editor of the ... "was of Kinderhook": "Daniel Van Tassel Gives the Results of His Investigation of Many Years," *New York Times*, May 28, 1898.

Brom Bones, Church Clerk: In 1797 ... "without any donation": C. E. Bacon, "Annals of the First Reformed," 10.

Brom Bones, Church Clerk: "No longer ... newly immortalized": E. M. Bacon, *Chronicles of Tarrytown*, 117.

CHAPTER 7
Page 97

"Revolutions would do well ... none of them": E. M. Bacon, *Chronicles of Tarrytown*, 50.

Pages 98–99

After fifteen years ... devouring tongue! Stewart, *Historical Discourse*, 160.

Pages 99

Afterward he taught ... was licensed by the Associated Presbyterian Church: Presbyterian and Reformed churches stem from the same Calvinist Protestant tradition.

Page 100

Though Jemima ... "manifestly unbalanced": from *Two Hundredth Anniversary*, 163.

Mourning the loss ... "loved so well": extract from the proceedings of the New York Classis meeting, April 18, 1837 (see *Two Hundredth Anniversary*, 169).

A Curious Resolution: Gerald G. Beekman ... the church: C. E. Bacon, "Annals of the First Reformed," 14.

Page 101

(Caption) Rev. Thomas Smith drew crowds ... as Smith called him: Stewart, *Historical Discourse*, 30.

Pipes ran from ... if necessary: Allen, *Old Dutch Church of Sleepy Hollow*, 1918, 15.

Page 102

He accepted under ... built in Tarrytown: C. E. Bacon, *"Annals of the First Reformed,"* 11.

Abraham and Julia Storms ... the next year: Manderen, *"Old Dutch Church"* address, 2–3.

Pages 102–103

Almost as if ... into flames: William Pfeifer's report to the consistory on the structure and current condition of the Old Dutch Church (January 17, 1985) includes the tradition that in 1837 lightning struck the church and it was damaged by fire; also, a school composition dated Sept. 30, 1841, (in church files) mentions the fire.

Page 103

"When we consider that the new church ... depression that followed": C. E. Bacon, *"Annals of the First Reformed,"* 12.

Other repairs may have altered the roofline, William Pfeifer, report to consistory (January 17, 1985), 3; also see notes for page 15.

Page 104

In any case ... "can be found": Stewart, *Historical Discourse,* 15.

"When the workmen had finished ... general appreciation": ibid., 17.

For the double duty, the consistory ... Rev. Smith's salary: E. M. Bacon, *Chronicles of Tarrytown,* 58.

Page 105

To finance the upkeep of two churches ... totaled $906: Manderen, "Old Dutch Church" address, 3.

Although other churches had sprung up ... Methodist and Catholic churches: Historical Society of the Tarrytowns Historic Church Tour brochure, May 20, 1979.

He quickly realized the attendance ... old church building: Stewart, *Historical Discourse,* 38.

Pages 105–106

What happened next? At two-thirty ... Indeed that church would prosper: Jack R. Hornady, Second Reformed Church booklet, "The Second Reformed Church, 1851–1976."

Page 106

Of 150 members remaining ... half enough to obtain for you even a parsonage: Stewart, *Historical Discourse,* 40–41.

Page 107

Pocantico Mission: By tradition, Sunday school ... gallery: E. M. Bacon says in *Chronicles of Tarrytown,* 58, that the Sunday school of the old church met at Old Dutch in 1837–38.

Pocantico Mission: In the summer ... in the churchyard: Rev. John Bodine Thompson, report on "The Pocantico Mission," church records.

Page 108

The Remarkable Reverend: A persistent legend ... safe house on the route: Conklin, *Historical Tarrytown,* 33.

The Remarkable Reverend: A band ... turning them back: E. M. Bacon, *Chronicles of Tarrytown,* 63–64.

CHAPTER 8
Page 112

"I had to take the time ... to our common country": Roosevelt speech Oct. 11, 1897, www.theodore-roosevelt.com/images/research/txtspeeches/779.pdf.

Page 113

By 1985, however, the Old Dutch ... in a masonry wall: State Preservation Project Application, church files.

In a plea for community support ... "beginning of this community": Jonathan Bandler, "Historic Church Not Free From Village Permit Fee," *Gannett Suburban Newspapers/Westchester,* July 8, 1991.

Contributions soon arrived ... topped up the fund: former church treasurer Vito Addotta.

Said Joanne Addotta, "We have an original ... the way it was: Pamela Schaeffer, "Old East Church No Match for Hi-Tech Cousin in West," Aug. 12, 1991, Religious News Service.

Page 117

Proposals to reunite ... were floated in 1914: C. E. Bacon, *"Annals of the First Reformed,"* 23.

An air of excitement ... Catherine and Frederick Philipse: Josh Kurtz, "Two Old Churches of the Tarrytowns Come Together," *New York Times,* Feb. 17, 1991.

Page 123

Long May the Little Church Stand! essay from "The Legendary History of the Old Dutch Church of Sleepy Hollow," by Rev. John Knox Allen, D.D., Tarrytown Historical Society, 1918, 33–34.

"Ring in the valiant man ... that is to be," Alfred, Lord Tennyson, "In Memoriam A.H.H.," 1849.

ILLUSTRATIONS

HHV—Historic Hudson Valley; **LOC**—Library of Congress Prints and Photographs Division; **NYHS**—New-York Historical Society; **RCT**—Reformed Church of the Tarrytowns; **WCHS**—Westchester County Historical Society

Front Cover: Old Dutch Church of Sleepy Hollow, by Frank Van Steen, 1971, courtesy Frank and Marjorie Van Steen Foundation

PHOTOGRAPHS

PERSONAL NOTES

PERSONAL NOTES

PERSONAL NOTES

PERSONAL NOTES

Long May the Little Church Stand!

The following extract was written nearly a hundred years ago, in 1918, by Rev. John Knox Allen, D.D., the minister of First Reformed Church. His words still ring true today.

"It is as hard for us to conceive the state of things which shall be two hundred years from now as it is to imagine what was two hundred years ago. On what a teeming life, on what a changed world, will the little spire then look down! The Hudson and the hills will be unchanged, but what else? Certain it is that we shall seem as shadowy and unreal to the men of that coming time as now these figures of the past are to us. Perchance some antiquarian near the birth hour of the twenty-second century will turn over the musty records of the same church, and with his glass make out from the almost faded ink the name of the writer of this paper, and wonder who on earth he was, and what on earth he did.

"Long may the little church stand, binding the present to a noble past.... And through many successive summers may the little bell which has feebly tolled the passing of so many souls, and called so many of the living to listen to what it could not say, tinkle in its tower; may it continue to ring until it shall toll the world's sin to its burial, and announce the final Sabbath, the day of rest after the world's long toil and sorrow." Rev. Allen then quoted a Tennyson poem:

"RING IN THE VALIANT MAN AND FREE, THE LARGER HEART, THE KINDLIER HAND; RING OUT THE DARKNESS OF THE LAND, RING IN THE CHRIST THAT IS TO BE."

Photo: Good Friday Service, 2011, by Jim Logan.